In *Idols of a Mother's Heart*  wealth of wisdom and th exposes the idols we often b comfort, achievement, and the problem in our own hearts. Most Christina points to the grace of God by encouraging mothers to turn from idolatry and find life in Christ alone.

Melissa Kruger

Author of *In All Things: A Nine-Week Devotional Bible Study on Unshakeable Joy,* and *The Envy of Eve*

As parents, we never intentionally set out to shift God's good gifts from their rightful place to an ultimate place in our hearts. Idolatry can be subtle or flagrant but either way what we need is heart surgery. *Idols of a Mother's Heart* brings the gentle scalpel of the gospel to the divided hearts of women. Every page is Scripture saturated and theologically robust. I found myself praying, 'Lord change my heart, and change the hearts of women so that their lives, homes, churches, and communities exalt You alone as preeminent!'

Karen Hodge

Coordinator, Women's Ministry, Presbyterian Church in America

In *Idols of a Mother's Heart*, Christina Fox provides a study that is rich in biblical truth and practical application. She skillfully weaves together Bible texts, quotes from helpful authors, and her own personal experiences to create a picture of the struggles every mother faces as well as the hope found in the gospel. The discussion questions at the end of every chapter serve as a great catalyst for deeper reflection and valuable discussion. Each chapter also closes with a prayer that leads the reader to see the topic in the light of a holy and gracious God. This book is a great resource for mothers who are eager to fulfill their calling to glorify and enjoy God.

Stephen T. Estock
Coordinator, Christian Discipleship Ministries, Presbyterian Church in America

Page by page, Christina Fox peels back the layers of a mother's heart, helping her pluck out idols until there is nothing left but the grace of God. *Idols of a Mother's Heart* is a convicting surgery of the soul, as Fox delicately deals with our rogue, wild hearts, continually pointing us back to the transforming work of Jesus Christ—the only one worthy of our worship. With penetrating questions, humble honesty, and gospel freedom on every page, this book will not only stretch and challenge a mother, but point her to the joy and satisfaction found in her Savior alone.

Laura Wifler
Co-Founder of Risen Motherhood

Christina Fox's heart is on every page as she longs for moms to have a right view of how God sees them. With the gentle nudge of a friend, Christina encourages women to enter into mothering from the only safe place—rest and fullness in Christ.

Holly Mackle
Author of *Same Here, Sisterfriend: Mostly True Tales of Misadventures in Motherhood* and *Little Hearts, Prepare Him Room.*

I always enjoy reading what Christina Fox writes. Her books are thoughtful, clear, practical, and full of the riches of Scripture. *Idols of a Mother's Heart* is no different. With gentle precision, Fox exposes the lesser gods that take up residence in our hearts. And, with wisdom born of personal experience, she helps readers tear them down— so that Christ might have His rightful place. Mothers, if you want to learn to hate sin and love Christ, this book is for you.

Megan Hill
Editor, The Gospel Coalition,
editorial board, Christianity Today,
author of *Praying Together*

I recently spent two hours in the dentist's chair getting a tooth extracted because I had neglected to go to the dentist for work on a decaying tooth. Instead of a somewhat uncomfortable 30-minute procedure to fill and preserve the tooth, I had two hours of excruciating pulling, pushing, sawing, drilling, etc., and now I take twice as long to eat a steak. Christina's book on the idols of a mother's heart will cause you some short-term spiritual discomfort, but it is essentially preservative work and will ultimately not only save you far more pain in the long run but will fill your soul with much good and healthy nourishment.

David Murray
Professor of Old Testament and Practical Theology, Puritan
Reformed Theological Seminary,
author of *Jesus on Every Page*, *Reset: Living a Grace-Paced Life in a
Burnout Culture*, and *Exploring the Bible*

IDOLS
of a
MOTHER'S
HEART

CHRISTIAN
FOCUS

Copyright © Christina Fox 2018

paperback ISBN 978-1-5271-0233-0
epub ISBN 978-1-5271-0286-6
mobi ISBN 978-1-5271-0287-3

First published in 2018
by
Christian Focus Publications Ltd,
Geanies House, Fearn, Ross-shire
IV20 1TW, Scotland

www.christianfocus.com

A CIP catalogue record for this book is available from the British Library.

Cover design by Pete Barnsley

Printed and bound by Bell and Bain, Glasgow

CONTENTS

To Lisa, Marilyn, and Cara.
Thanks for journeying with me in the early years of
motherhood

ACKNOWLEDGMENTS

The Apostle Paul described the church as being a body made up of many parts. Some parts are more in the forefront and noticeable, while others are not. In a similar way, when it comes to writing a book, while my name is on the cover, many other people help make it possible.

Thanks to Christian Focus for taking on this project. I have enjoyed working with the MacKenzies and their team and am grateful for their diligence and work on this book.

I am thankful to Dr Stephen Estock and his leadership, wisdom, and guidance. I enjoy working with his team at CDM as editor of enCourage and assisting in other discipleship projects. I am especially grateful for his help in reading and giving me theological guidance on this book.

Thanks to Megan Hill for her friendship and partnership in prayer. She is an encouragement to me in writing and I am thankful for her editorial assistance and generous wisdom on this project.

Thanks also to Lisa Tarplee for her gospel friendship and assistance in reading the manuscript. Her eye to detail and gift of creativity is an asset to me.

Thanks to Pastor Paul at ECPC for reading the manuscript and sharing your wisdom with me. I am grateful for the spiritual shepherding and leadership at my church.

Karen Hodge, thank you for your continued mentorship in ministry, encouragement in writing, and support. I am grateful for you!

Thanks to all my readers. Thank you for reading my books, articles, and posts and sharing your stories with me. You are an encouragement to me.

A special thanks goes to my family—George, Ethan, and Ian—for their constant prayers and encouragement. They are always understanding of the space and time I need to write and I am so grateful for their sacrifice.

To my fellow moms and friends in the trenches who provide prayer, encouragement, and support: Lisa Tarplee, Marilyn Southwick, Cara Leger, Holly Mackle, Maryanne Helms, Debbie Locke, Amy Masters, Becky Jackson, Jen Acklen, and all the Loft Ladies—thank you!

Most of all, I am thankful to the Lord for using me despite my weaknesses and failings, for His steadfast mercy and grace toward me, and His hand of providence in all the details of my life. I never expected to write one book, and certainly not three! The writing process is humbling and sanctifying and I'm thankful for the ways in which the Lord uses writing in my growth in holiness.

INTRODUCTION

When my children were little, I invited a small group of moms to meet at my house each week. We read a book together, discussed it, and prayed together. We were all in the same stage of life: early motherhood. Our children were under five years of age and we were knee deep in childcare, exhaustion, and parenting dilemmas. We often felt helpless and insufficient to the task of motherhood. Those weekly meetings kept us grounded and helped us realize we weren't alone. We prayed with and for each other, spurring one another on in the faith.

One of the books we read together was Tim Keller's *Counterfeit Gods*. It was eye-opening for me. I hadn't studied the topic of idolatry in depth before. It helped me see that idolatry is more than worship of a statue or the love of money. *Counterfeit Gods* helped me see how even good things can become idols. Because my life was centered on motherhood, I found myself reading the book and relating the idols Keller described in the book to my life as a mother. I could see ways in which I worshipped success as a mother. I saw how I looked for life, purpose, and meaning in motherhood. I realized I worshipped control in the ways I sought to order, structure, and command the chaos of life.

As a result, I ended up writing an article for Desiring God Ministries, titled, 'The Idols of a Mother's Heart.' It was about idols specific to motherhood. The article ended up in the book *Mom Enough: The Fearless Mother's Heart and Hope.*

I knew there was more I wanted to explore and learn from this topic and am thankful that Christian Focus gave me the opportunity to write a book about it.

This book is something you can't breeze through. You need to take your time. Be thoughtful and prayerful about your own heart as you read. Pray for wisdom and discernment. Pray that you will have spiritual insight to see the idols you worship. And pray for God's grace to transform you in the process, because isn't that what we need most of all? Learning about idolatry is one thing. But having mere knowledge doesn't change our lives. We need the Holy Spirit to work in us and change us. We need the truths we read to intersect with our hearts, changing us from the inside out. Only God can do that deep surgical work. Prayer is an integral part of identifying idolatry in our lives and rooting it out, so I encourage you to be in prayer throughout the reading of this book.

What You Can Expect

The first chapter is about motherhood. All mothers know how challenging motherhood can be. Whatever expectations we had at the start of our journey in motherhood were quickly dashed after we first held our child in our arms. Motherhood has stretched us in ways we never saw coming. But just like physical stretching, though it makes us sore, it is for our good. God uses motherhood, as another of many means, to sanctify us and chapter 1 discusses that truth.

Chapters 2-4 are about idolatry. In chapter 2, we look at how we were created to worship and what happened to our worship in the Fall. In chapter 3, we explore idolatry and its impact on the heart. In chapter 4, I identify specific questions you can ask your own heart to help you see and evaluate the idols you worship.

Chapters 5-9 focus on a few different idols that mothers might worship. These are not all the idols mothers have; I've just chosen a common few. As you read, explore your heart, and pray through the chapters. And as you do, other idols might come to your attention.

The final chapters are about facing idols, dethroning them, and turning our heart back to the one true God.

I encourage you to read this book with other moms and explore idolatry together in community as I did with my discipleship group. I've included discussion questions, Scripture readings and prayers at the end of each chapter to help you in personal reflection and in group discussion.

Don't Waste the Season of Motherhood

Moms, we all find unique and different challenges in motherhood. Mine are probably different from yours and yours are different from another mom friend of yours. Some days are harder than others. Some weeks are joy-filled and others are more than you can handle. These years of raising children and helping them grow in the nurture and admonition of the Lord provide an opportunity for us to grow as well. See the hardships, challenges, weaknesses, and frustrations as a place for God to work in you, transforming and sanctifying you by His grace.

When my kids were little, older women would tell me how fast the season of motherhood passes and to enjoy every minute of it. Looking back, I agree with them. Not only should we enjoy the precious few moments we have with our children, we also need to seize the opportunities for our own growth during this season. Let's not waste the season of motherhood. Each late night visit from a little one, every tantrum in the middle of the grocery store, each disruption to our routine, and every unexpected illness is an opportunity for God to show us our need for Him. He alone is our salvation and our life. Hard as we try, we cannot find life outside of Him.

Will you join me in this journey?

In Christ,

Christina Fox

PART 1

MOTHERHOOD, WORSHIP, AND IDOLATRY

1

THE SANCTIFYING WORK OF MOTHERHOOD

Every mom has a birth story to tell. Whether it's a baby's birth in a hospital or a baby birthed in the heart through adoption, we all have a story. When we gather together as women, we tell those stories. We share the dramatic events, and sometimes even the gory details surrounding our child's birth, just like a soldier recounts his time on the front lines of war.

I've heard stories of women delivering their baby in the car, right outside the emergency room entrance of the hospital. I've heard stories of women delivering babies in their bathtub at home. I once attended a friend's home-birth—which was amazing! I've known friends who have delivered the tiniest of babies and then had to wait months before they could finally bring them home. I've listened to stories of moms who filled out reams of papers, overcame one obstacle after another, and traveled thousands of miles to another country to finally hold their child in their arms.

While motherhood begins with a birth story, there are many more stories that make up the life of a mother. Moment by moment, day after day, a mother's story is unfolding as she loves, nurtures, raises, and trains her children. Each of these moments make up the bigger story God is writing about each of us. The focus of motherhood is often on caring for and raising a child. Yet the bigger story, the story we'll look back on and be most amazed by, is the story of what God did in and through us as mothers—how He used motherhood to change and transform us more into the likeness of Christ.

What this means is, the mom at the beginning of the story is the not the same one at the end.

On Motherhood and Whirlwinds

I too have a birth story. And while I will cut out the gory details, I will share part of the story. Here is how I often begin: *A hurricane made me a mother and it's been a whirlwind ever since.*

It was the fall of 2004. Two category-three hurricanes crashed into our small coastal town in the space of a few weeks. I was just nine months pregnant. It was unbearably hot, as every September is in South Florida. I was uncomfortable—as all mothers-to-be are—and counted down the days until I could see my toes again.

I spent the first hurricane holed up at my in-laws' house a couple of hours away while my husband reported for duty at the fire station. Before I made the drive to my in-laws' house, I talked to my doctor and discussed where I would go in case I had the baby while I was out of town. The hurricane was a large storm; it took a couple of days to cross the state. I waited, stressed and anxious, wondering—will this be the day? Will I have my son here, during the storm?

When the storm passed over us and I was still with child, I returned home. My car was filled with boxes and boxes of everything we held dear (mostly photo albums—remember those?). A couple of weeks later, we heard news that another storm was on its way. I couldn't believe it! My due date was days away. Really, Lord? Another storm?

This time, when the second category-three hurricane rolled onshore, my husband, myself, and a couple of other families gathered in the home of a friend to wait it out. We were prepared for an obstetrical emergency: my husband had an OB kit from the fire station and one of our friends was a nurse.

Thankfully, I made it through the storm without any emergencies but the following night my water broke. The problem was, I had to deliver a baby in a town devastated by two hurricanes. The power was out everywhere. Half of the hospital was damaged. People recovering from surgery were taken to the maternity ward, along with lots of other women who went into labor as a result of the storm. Women labored in beds lining the hallways. Needless to say, the staff and doctors were stretched thin.

I had complications after the birth and had to stay in the hospital a few days longer. Everything was chaos around me as exhausted doctors and nurses worked overtime, all the while wondering about the state of their homes after the storm. I wasn't allowed to sit up in bed and had to lie still for three days, making it hard to handle a newborn. I remember thinking, 'Nothing went the way it was supposed to go. Nothing happened the way I expected.'

Everything Changes

A baby changes everything. That's what they say anyway. And in many ways, it's true.

When I first learned I was expecting, I immediately went to the bookstore and bought *What to Expect When You're Expecting*. It was the bible for expectant mothers. I read it cover to cover. It described every change a woman can expect in her body during the nine months of pregnancy. It also described in great detail what to expect during childbirth and the few weeks after. I followed that book day by day and week by week, comparing the changes in my body to what the book described.

Some changes a woman experiences in pregnancy are obvious. For women who become mothers through childbirth, the first changes are physical. Expectant moms often stand in front of a mirror, hold up their shirt, and look for the 'baby bump.' Before long, other people notice it and congratulate her. As the months go by, her belly grows bigger and bigger. This is an obvious change. The stretch marks that mar her skin are another. Her fluctuating tastes and desire for food (or lack thereof) is yet another change. For the rest of her life, her bladder never functions the same way again.

Those are physical changes, but there are other changes as well. Whether a woman carries a baby nine months in her womb or many months (sometimes years) in her heart through adoption, there are changes all moms experience. Some changes include loss of sleep and energy, giving up her personal space, having less time and money, and even the 'mommy brain' syndrome I still claim today. (You know, the phenomenon where you walk into a room and forget why you are there, or when you put the milk back into the pantry instead of in the refrigerator.) A mother also has a new person to care for and be responsible for: her baby is dependent upon her in a way no one has ever been. When she makes decisions about how she uses her time and resources, she has to factor in her child.

Another change a mother experiences is that of love. The love she has for her child is unlike anything she's experienced. It is a protective love. A fierce love. A love that somehow senses what her child needs before even the child knows it. A mother experiences a sacrificial love, the kind that would give anything and do anything for her child.

One Thing Remains the Same

There is much that changes in our lives when we become a mother, but one thing that doesn't change is the problem of sin. It's been a problem since the day Adam and Eve disobeyed God in the Garden and has remained with us ever since. Such sin broke Adam and Eve's communion with God and each other, expelled them from the Garden, and brought sin and death to all things. Romans 3:23 tells us that 'all have sinned and fall short of the glory of God.' Every human is born a sinner. Sin is part of our makeup as humans, inherited from our first parents. This is why David wrote: 'Behold, I was brought forth in iniquity, and in sin did my mother conceive me' (Ps. 51:5).

While Adam was our representative in the Garden, Jesus became our representative in His perfect life and sacrificial death on the cross. For us who by faith trust in Christ as our Savior, God looks at us and sees not our sin, but the righteousness of Christ. Our sins have been forgiven; we've been cleansed and made new. (We'll talk more about this process of being made new in a bit.) Through Christ's atoning work for us on the cross, we've been set free from the power of sin—it no longer owns us. However, the presence of sin still remains. If you are a new Christian, you might have noticed that you still have that nagging problem of sin in your life. It didn't go away, did it? The difference is, rather than it being the *only* thing you can do, through the power of the Holy Spirit at work in you now you are able to *not* sin. Now you are able to want what God wants. For Christians, sin is no longer our master and we are no longer its slave. But it continues to reside in us. We spend our lives putting our sin to death. And we will do so until we die or Christ returns.

I don't know about you, but when I was expecting my first child and thinking about what motherhood would be like, I didn't factor in the problem of sin and what its impact would be on my mothering. Before I became a mom, I pictured motherhood to be like the sweet mother and baby interactions I saw on baby shampoo commercials. I imagined cuddles, smiles, laughter, and fun memories. When I daydreamed about motherhood, I pictured myself instructing with wisdom, responding with patience, and always handing out smiles.

And while there are certainly plenty of smiles, cuddles, and laughter, there is also the problem of sin. It impacts every aspect of our mothering. There's the impact of sin on creation, causing sickness, disease, and other health and developmental problems in our children. There's the sin of others and our responses to their sin—such as unkind children on the playground picking on our child or a shopper at the store who is quick to point out our failings as a mother. There's the sin of our children, their willfulness and desire for their own way. And of course, there's our own sin. From our impatient and angry responses, to reactionary discipline, to expecting more from them than they are capable of, to simply failing to make wise choices in our parenting, we can see sin in all areas of our motherhood.

It doesn't take much for my sin to make an appearance. Just this morning, I was enjoying a cup of dark roast and reading my Bible before the day got away from me. In the middle of my reading, I heard footsteps pounding down the stairs and the word, 'Mom!' yelled at the top of my son's lungs. I breathed out a loud sigh and responded with an irritable tone of voice, 'What!' (While you can't hear it here, trust me, it was irritable.) The truth was, I didn't like the interruption to my peace and quiet and my tone made that very clear.

On a daily basis, as our sin clashes with our children's sin, it's just plain messy. Add our husband's sin to the mix and whoever else lives in our home with us, and it's a miracle that anyone has survived since the days of Adam and Eve!

Motherhood is Hard

It had been one of those 'terrible, horrible, no good, very bad days.' The kind where nothing went the way it should. I must have corrected the kids every five minutes. I refereed fights, cleaned up mess after mess, repeated instructions, and tried to create order out of chaos. I was exhausted, irritated, and impatient.

Sitting at the dinner table that evening, it was my oldest son's turn to give thanks. When I heard him say, 'And God, could you please help Mommy to be patient with us?' I realized I wasn't the only one affected by our difficult day. I was part of the problem too.[1]

While the *What to Expect* book prepared me for a lot of things about motherhood, it failed to highlight how hard it is. Unlike hard and difficult jobs I've had before, motherhood is all consuming. It consumes energy, time, emotions, wisdom, and everything else. It's a 24/7 job, without any breaks, holidays, or vacations. It challenges us in our weakest areas. It reveals our insufficiencies. It shows us just how much we don't know and how incapable we really are. And, it seems to spotlight sin in our heart, magnifying it so that we see the depths of our sin in ways we've never noticed before.

It's not as though motherhood *makes* us more of a sinner. Rather, areas of sin we didn't realize we had are brought to the surface. Sinful habits and patterns are brought to light that may have once been in the shadows. The pressures,

---

1. See an article I wrote titled, 'Parenting is Hard for a Reason' at The Gospel Coalition: https://www.thegospelcoalition.org/article/parenting-is-hard-for-a-reason/ (accessed May 16, 2018).

challenges, and difficulties of motherhood somehow make the sin we already have more pronounced. It's like when the sunlight streams through the windows at just the right angle and shines upon the furniture. That light reveals all the dust layered on the tabletop. It was there before, we just didn't notice it until the light shone down on it. In a similar way, specific areas of sin in our heart are brought out into the light in motherhood in ways they never had been before. We learn and realize new layers and depths of sin we didn't notice were there.

For example, we might come face to face with our impatience or irritability. Before motherhood we might not have been the most patient person in the world, but after motherhood, we learn just how impatient we actually are. Or motherhood might highlight a struggle with sins such as worry or sarcasm. A propensity we already had for worry might be magnified in motherhood—probably because there are so many reasons to worry! Motherhood might also reveal just how much we like things to be a certain way—our way. For some, motherhood may shine a light on sins we've kept buried down deep in the dark recesses of our heart. Being a mom reveals in a unique way the true nature of our heart. And like the dirty diapers we change each day, it isn't pretty.

Motherhood and Sanctification

But there's good news in the midst of the bad. While motherhood shines a spotlight on our sin, it is not outside God's perfect plan for us. In fact, these sins we notice, we notice them because the Spirit is at work in us revealing those sins to us. Our eyes are opened to see our chronic worry or desire for control or some hidden sin, maybe for the first time. These sins become opportunities for us to learn and grow and be changed into the likeness of Christ.

Theologians call this process of transformation 'sanctification.' The word sanctification means to be set apart. It is the process by which God changes us into the image of Christ. Theologians often point out that the Scriptures describe two aspects of sanctification. One is called *positional sanctification* which describes what happens at salvation when God declares us righteous in Christ. 'God sanctifies sinners once and for ever when he brings them to himself, separating them from the world, delivering them from sin and Satan, and welcoming them into his fellowship.'[2] The second aspect to sanctification is that of *progressive sanctification* where we are gradually 'changed more and more in mind and heart and life into the image of the Lord Jesus Christ.'[3]

Progressive sanctification is a process, a lifelong one at that. It's a work in which we are an active participant, but it is ultimately God's work. 'Therefore, my beloved, as you have always obeyed, so now, not only as in my presence but much more in my absence, work out your own salvation with fear and trembling, *for it is God who works in you, both to will and to work for his good pleasure*' (Phil. 2:12-13, emphasis mine). Paul describes this process as putting off and putting on: 'to put off your old self, which belongs to your former manner of life and is corrupt through deceit-

---

2. Packer, J.I., *God's Words* (Grand Rapids, MI: Baker Book House, 1988), p. 177.

3. Ibid., p. 178.

ful desires, and to be renewed in the spirit of your minds, and to put on the new self, created after the likeness of God in true righteousness and holiness' (Eph. 4:22-24). It is a co-operative work where we work along with the Holy Spirit in the process. As R.C. Sproul wrote, 'The call to cooperation is one that involves work. We are to work in earnest... We are consoled by the knowledge that we are not left to do this work alone or by our own efforts. God is working within us to accomplish our sanctification.'[4]

Just like salvation, sanctification is a work of God's grace, where He trains us: 'For the grace of God has appeared, bringing salvation for all people, training us to renounce ungodliness and worldly passions, and to live self-controlled, upright, and godly lives in the present age' (Titus 2:11-12). How amazing is God's grace! He saves us by grace, trains us by grace, and purifies us by grace. This ought to give us hope, knowing that God rules over the process and the end result doesn't rest or rely on us. Ultimately, it is the Holy Spirit's job to conform us into the image of Christ; He is the one who makes us holy.

For those who have been believers for any length of time, we know this process is not easy. Sometimes it's hard. Sometimes it's downright painful. As the Spirit reveals our sin to us and works in us to weed out those sins, it often hurts. Some of those sins have deep roots which have entangled themselves around our heart, like a vine around a tree. If you've ever had vines cover trees in

---

4. Sproul, R.C., *Essential Truths of the Christian Faith* (Wheaton, IL: Tyndale Publishing, 1998), p. 124.

your yard, you know it takes a lot of work to remove them. So it is with sin.

One of my favorite images of this process comes from *The Voyage of the Dawn Treader* by C.S. Lewis. The *Dawn Treader* is the name of a ship owned by Caspian, King of Narnia. He went on a journey to find the lost lords of Narnia. Lucy, Edmund, and their cousin Eustace joined Caspian in his journey. At one point in their voyage, while their ship was anchored at an island, Eustace wandered off from everyone else to do his own thing. He found a cave filled with gold and treasures and in his greed, desired it for himself. As a result, he turned into a dragon, covered in scales. 'He had turned into a dragon while he was asleep. Sleeping on a dragon's hoard with greedy, dragonish thoughts in his heart, he had become a dragon himself.'[5]

Aslan later found Eustace and removed the dragon skin from him. It was quite painful but it changed him from a dragon and back into a boy again. 'The very first tear he made was so deep that I thought it had gone right into my heart. And when he began pulling the skin off, it hurt worse than anything I've ever felt. The only thing that made me able to bear it was just the pleasure of feeling the stuff peel off.'[6]

The author to the Hebrews says this about the process of shedding our sin,

> It is for discipline that you have to endure. God is treating you as sons. For what son is there whom his father does

---

5. Lewis, C.S., *The Voyage of the Dawn Treader* (New York, NY: Macmillan, 1952), p. 75.

6. Ibid., p. 90.

not discipline? If you are left without discipline, in which all have participated, then you are illegitimate children and not sons. Besides this, we have had earthly fathers who disciplined us and we respected them. Shall we not much more be subject to the Father of spirits and live? For they disciplined us for a short time as it seemed best to them, but he disciplines us for our good, that we may share his holiness. For the moment all discipline seems painful rather than pleasant, but later it yields the peaceful fruit of righteousness to those who have been trained by it (Heb. 12:7-11).

Yes, the process of sanctification is painful, but it comes from the hand of our loving Father. It is an evidence of our adoption as God's children. While our earthly parents disciplined us as they thought best, God's discipline is perfect and right. He does it for our good so that we would grow in holiness. Consider your own children. Perhaps you have a daughter who loves candy but the dentist has warned you not to give it to her. Your child asks you for a lollipop that the bank teller has sitting in a bowl just within reach and you tell her she can't have it. It's for her own good, but to a child who does not yet understand the long-term consequences of candy consumption, it is not good. To her, it seems mean. Likewise, we often question God's discipline, failing to see the long-term work He is doing in us. But we can be assured that His discipline is good and it will produce holiness in us.

A couple of years ago, I developed a bad habit of typing on my laptop while sitting on the couch. I wrote much of a book this way. The problem was, the position of my hands caused injury to the tendon in my arm: I developed tendinitis or what's commonly called 'tennis elbow.' My doctor sent me to an orthopedist who ordered physical therapy.

I went to the physical therapist and the exercises the therapist gave me to do were painful. He also poked and prodded and dug his fingers deep into my arm. It was excruciating! But as my therapist said in response to my protests, 'I'm sorry, I know this hurts but it's what we have to do to heal your arm.' In order for my arm to heal, I had to endure more pain. Several months later, I realized he was right because my arm had healed. It's a trite saying, but 'no pain, no gain' is true. It's also true when it comes to our growth in holiness, our sanctification. We often have to endure the pain of discipline or the pain of having our sin stripped away in order to grow in Christ's likeness.

In the process of sanctification, we may find two seemingly contradictory things happening. As we move farther along in the faith, we will find ourselves making progress in putting sin to death. Some sins we struggled with in our younger days of faith might not be a problem for us. We'll find ourselves no longer desiring things that displease God. While at the same time, the closer we grow in our love and faith for our holy, righteous God, the more we realize we are not holy and righteous as He is. The Apostle Paul, as he grew in his own faith, moved from describing himself as the least of the disciples (1 Cor. 15:9) to the least of the saints (Eph. 3:8) to the chief of all sinners (1 Tim. 1:15). The more he knew Christ, the more he saw his sinfulness. It's not that he became more sinful, it's just that he grew in his understanding of the depths of his sin.

Perhaps we can compare it to my sunlight analogy from earlier. Often, I will dust a table and then later, as the sun starts to set in the evening and the light shines across the top of the table, I realize just how much dust is still there. While I removed dust when I cleaned, the sunlight revealed there was still more there. In a similar way, while I am making progress in my fight against sin, the more I grow in my knowledge of God, the more He reveals to me layers of sin I hadn't noticed before. In truth, it's just another aspect of His grace toward me that He doesn't reveal all my sin to me at once—who could bear it? He slowly makes me more and more aware of my desperate need for Him. And at the same time, He enables me to continue to fight and strive in His strength to put sin to death.

Our process of sanctification will not be completed in this life. We'll make great progress as we move forward in our journey, but we won't see the finished product until we step into eternity. 'And I am sure of this, that he who began a good work in you will bring it to completion at the day of Jesus Christ' (Phil. 1:6). On that day, we will shed our sin once and for all. We will be like Christ and see Him as He is (1 John 3:2).

So what does all of this have to do with motherhood? First, as mothers, we all face the problem of the presence of remaining sin in our life. Secondly, motherhood is hard. It is challenging and stretching in unique ways, different from other areas of our life. Thirdly, motherhood is another area of our life God uses to transform us. While He uses other circumstances, roles, and places in our life—marriage, work, sickness, suffering, relationships, even getting stuck in traffic—to change and refine us, He also uses motherhood. As mothers, we ought to view the difficulties and challenges we face in our mothering as opportunities to learn, grow, obey, and be changed more into the likeness of Christ.

As we move through this book, we are going to focus on the idols of our heart. Idolatry is a sin that often reveals itself in unique ways in our motherhood. Consider the pages which lie ahead as an opportunity, an opportunity to see the things that need to be 'put off' in your life. It is also an opportunity to grow in our dependency and reliance upon the God who not only saved us by grace, but transforms us by His grace. And because it's God's work in us, we can expect great things to come from it.

Questions for a Mother's Heart:

1. How would you compare your expectation of motherhood with your actual experience of it?

2. Have you noticed specific sins come to the forefront since becoming a mother? Which ones?

3. Read 2 Corinthians 3:18. What does it mean by 'unveiled faces'? How did our faces become unveiled? Who does the transforming?

4. Read Galatians 5:22-25. What can you expect the Spirit to develop in you as you are sanctified?

5. Read Colossians 1:9-14. Make this your personal prayer as you go through this book.

A Prayer for a Mother's Heart:

Dear Father,

I come before you today weary and worn. Motherhood is harder than I expected. I feel weak and insufficient. My heart is filled with worries about my children. I often just don't know what to do.

While this place of weakness and uncertainty is hard for me, I know it is a good place. I know you are with me and you are at work. I know that you are doing good things in my heart and even on my worst day, you are making me into the image of your Son

Forgive me for the ways I've tried to do life in my own strength. Forgive me for my worries and fears. Forgive me for not loving my family the way that you love me. Strengthen me by your grace to live for you. Help me to seek you. Help me to glorify you in my mothering.

In Jesus' name,

Amen.

2

MADE FOR WORSHIP

Before I became a mom, I loved sleep. I always have. I looked forward to weekends when I wouldn't have to set the alarm and could get up whenever I wanted. I could easily sleep ten hours if given the opportunity. Maybe more!

This love for sleep was challenged when I became a mom. Those first few months when my son was a newborn were hard. I slept between feedings during the night. I followed the night-time cycle mothers know all too well: feed, sleep an hour or two, and feed again. Repeat.

In the morning, I would calculate in my mind how many total hours of sleep I got from the interrupted sleep I was able to catch in between feedings. 'Six. That's not bad. You can make it on six,' I'd tell myself. Despite my pep talk, I couldn't make it. I was exhausted. Over time, I became obsessed with sleep. It was an elusive thing that always moved farther out of my reach. I strategized ways to get more. But even when I did lie down to sleep, the slightest noise would awaken me. Sometimes no matter how tired I was, I couldn't fall asleep. I told myself, 'If only I got a solid eight hours, I'd be a happier person; I'd be a better mom.'

You could say that I worshipped sleep.

In this chapter, we are going to look at worship. Because idolatry is about worship, we need to start at the beginning and see how God made us to worship and what happened to that worship.

Made for worship

Not many of us have time for existential thought or speculation. We don't generally sit around and muse about the meaning or purpose of life. We don't get together with friends, smoke pipes, and toss around quotes by Kierkegaard, Sartre, or Barth. If we did before motherhood, we certainly don't now!

But there's an important question we need to answer that builds the foundation for the topic of this book. And that question is: *Why were we created?*

As a child, I learned the shorter catechism of the Westminster Confession of Faith. Some of the questions I still remember and others I can only partially recite. But the first question is firmly entrenched in my mind and it is this: What is man's primary purpose? Or in the older version: What is the chief end of man? The answer is: *To glorify God and enjoy Him forever.*[1]

Isaiah 43:7 says, 'everyone who is called by my name, whom I created for my glory, whom I formed and made.' In this passage, God is talking specifically about the Israelites but note that He says 'whom I created for my glory.' 1 Corinthians 10:31 says that all we do in this life is for God's glory, 'So, whether you eat or drink, or whatever you do, do all to the glory of God.' The gifts He gives us are for His glory, 'As each has received a gift, use it to serve one another, as good stewards of God's varied grace: whoever speaks, as one who speaks oracles of God; whoever serves, as one who serves by the strength that God supplies—*in order that in everything God may be glorified through Jesus Christ*. To him belong glory and dominion forever and ever. Amen' (1 Pet. 4:10-11, emphasis mine). Even sorrows and other trials serve to glorify God (see John 9:3 and 11:4).

The reason God created us is so that we would bring Him glory. We were made to worship our Maker. The purpose of the church is to proclaim His glory throughout the world, 'Declare his glory among the nations, his marvelous works among all the peoples!' (Ps. 96:3). And one day, every knee will bow and confess Christ as Lord. One day, the whole earth will proclaim the glory of God. 'For the earth will be filled with the knowledge of the glory of the LORD as the waters cover the sea' (Hab. 2:14).

---

1. Williamson, G.I., *The Westminster Shorter Catechism: For Study Classes, Volume 1* (Phillipsburg, NJ: P&R Publishing Company, 2012), p.1.

Glorifying and Enjoying God

You might wonder, what does that even mean? How do we live to glorify God? To glorify God means that we reflect God's glory. When God created mankind, He created us as image bearers (see Gen. 1:26-27). An image bearer images the original, therefore we image the original—God. We reflect Him. We point to Him. We mirror Him.

When we look up at the moon in the night sky, it provides us light to see, especially when it's a full moon. Yet the moon has no light of its own. It merely reflects the light of the sun. That's what we do as image bearers, we reflect who God is. As R.C. Sproul put it, 'The task that is given to mankind in creation is to bear witness to the holiness of God, to be His image bearer. We are made to mirror and reflect the holiness of God. We are made to be His ambassadors.'[2]

John Piper describes glorifying God this way, 'glorifying means feeling and thinking and acting in ways that reflect his greatness, that make much of God, that give evidence of the supreme greatness of all his attributes and the all satisfying beauty of his manifold perfections.'[3] When we glorify God, we don't make Him glorious; He already is. When we glorify Him, we are showing or displaying or declaring God's glory. That's what the creation does, 'The heavens declare the glory of God, and the sky above proclaims his handiwork' (Ps. 19:1).

---

2. Sproul, R.C., *The Holiness of God* (Carol Stream, IL: Tyndale Publishing, 1985), p. 113.

3. Desiring God Ministries. http://www.desiringgod.org/messages /glorifying-god-period (accessed February 10, 2017).

We glorify God when we seek to reflect Him in all that we do—whether we eat or drink or anything else. It's what we do when we reflect Him in our work, by our diligence, creativity, and trustworthiness. We glorify Him when we are kind, truthful, and patient in our conversations with our children. We glorify Him when we drive safely on the road and don't respond in anger toward the person who pulls in front of us. When we show love to our children by reading them the same story over and over (and over!), we reflect God's great love and patience for us. No matter where we are and what we are doing, all of life is lived for the honor and glory of the One who made us.

The Westminster catechism question also says that we are to 'enjoy Him forever.' John Piper says that we glorify God *by* enjoying Him. As he wrote in *Desiring God*, 'God is most glorified in us when we are most satisfied in him.'[4] When we find our joy in knowing God and being known by Him, He is glorified. After all, God is the greatest treasure of all. He is the source and fountainhead of joy and happiness. So when we seek Him as our treasure and prize, we glorify Him. 'You make known to me the path of life; in your presence there is fullness of joy; at your right hand are pleasures forevermore' (Ps. 16:11).

It is important as moms that we remember our purpose in life, that we remember why we were created. In our daily life as moms, that purpose is often eclipsed by our busyness with the tasks of motherhood. We get wrapped up in the challenges, worries, and responsibilities of rais-

---

4. Piper, John., *Desiring God: Meditations of a Christian Hedonist* (Sisters, OR: Multnomah, 2003), p. 288.

ing our children. Remember this as we move forward: We were made for worship. We were made to glorify and enjoy our Maker.

God is Worthy

Not only is glorifying God and enjoying Him our chief end or purpose, but we glorify and enjoy Him because He is worthy. When we glorify Him, we are giving Him what He is due. As the twenty-four elders before the throne sing, 'Worthy are you, our Lord and God, to receive glory and honor and power, for you created all things, and by your will they existed and were created' (Rev. 4:11). And as Paul wrote in his doxology,

> Oh, the depth of the riches and wisdom and knowledge of God! How unsearchable are his judgments and how inscrutable his ways! 'For who has known the mind of the Lord, or who has been his counselor?' 'Or who has given a gift to him that he might be repaid?' For from him and through him and to him are all things. To him be glory forever. Amen (Rom. 11:33-36).

God is the Maker and Sustainer of all things. He is supreme and ruler over everything. He is sovereign; nothing happens outside of His knowledge and will. He knows all things and sees all things. He is everywhere: nothing can contain Him. He is all powerful: nothing and no one can control Him. He is the 'Alpha and the Omega, the first and the last, the beginning and the end' (Rev. 22:13). He is holy, righteous, and just. 'Righteous are you, O LORD, and right are your rules' (Ps. 119:137).

In the book of Isaiah, the prophet had a vision of heaven. He saw the Lord in His holiness.

> In the year that King Uzziah died I saw the Lord sitting upon a throne, high and lifted up; and the train of his robe filled the temple. Above him stood the seraphim. Each had six wings: with two he covered his face, and with two he covered his feet, and with two he flew. And one called to another and said: 'Holy, holy, holy is the LORD of hosts; the whole earth is full of his glory!' And the foundations of the thresholds shook at the voice of him who called, and the house was filled with smoke. And I said: 'Woe is me! For I am lost; for I am a man of unclean lips, and I dwell in the midst of a people of unclean lips; for my eyes have seen the King, the LORD of hosts!' (Isa. 6:1-5).

Can you imagine that? The sights and sounds Isaiah experienced were extraordinary! In seeing God on His throne as ruler of all things, Isaiah saw himself in contrast to the holiness and magnificence of God. He responded with, 'Woe is me!'

R.C. Sproul comments on this passage, 'In that single moment, all of his self-esteem was shattered. In a brief second he was exposed, made naked beneath the gaze of the absolute standard of holiness. As long as Isaiah could compare himself to other mortals, he was able to sustain a lofty opinion of his character. The instant he measured himself by the ultimate standard, he was destroyed—morally and spiritually annihilated. He was undone. He came apart.'[5] Later he wrote, 'For the first time in his life Isaiah

---

5. Sproul, R.C., p. 28.

really understood who God was. At the same instant, for the first time Isaiah really understood who Isaiah was.'[6]

Job also had an encounter with the holiness and power of God. Job questioned God after he suffered and lost nearly everything in his life. God's response was to remind Job of who He was: 'Then the LORD answered Job out of the whirlwind and said: "Who is this that darkens counsel by words without knowledge? ... Where were you when I laid the foundation of the earth? Tell me, if you have understanding. Who determined its measurements—surely you know! Or who stretched the line upon it? ... Have you commanded the morning since your days began, and caused the dawn to know its place ... Can you send forth lightnings, that they may go and say to you, 'Here we are'? Who has put wisdom in the inward parts or given understanding to the mind?"' (Job 38:1-2, 4-5, 12, 35-36). After two chapters of these questions, Job responded, 'Behold, I am of small account; what shall I answer you? I lay my hand on my mouth. I have spoken once, and I will not answer; twice, but I will proceed no further' (Job 40:4-5).

Here's yet another example. In Exodus 33, Moses asked to see God's glory. The problem was, no one could see God's glory and live. God told Moses to hide in the cleft of a rock and he could see God's glory from the back as He passed by. Exodus 34 recounts what God said when He passed by Moses, 'The LORD passed before him and proclaimed, "The LORD, the LORD, a God merciful and gracious, slow to anger, and abounding in steadfast love

---

6. Ibid., p. 29.

and faithfulness, keeping steadfast love for thousands, forgiving iniquity and transgression and sin, but who will by no means clear the guilty, visiting the iniquity of the fathers on the children and the children's children, to the third and the fourth generation." And Moses quickly bowed his head toward the earth and worshiped' (vv. 6-8).

All of these passages reveal that God is worthy. He is three times holy. They are powerful reminders for us as believers that God alone deserves all glory, honor, and praise. Every person who has encountered God's glory is left prostrate, silent, and undone. For us as moms, these passages are worth reading on a regular basis to remind ourselves of who God is. I don't know about you, but in the mundane tasks of my daily life, I often forget the magnificence of my Creator God. When all I see around me is nerf darts on the floor, crumbs on the table, and the laundry that still needs to be folded, I forget about the amazing God who cast the stars in the sky and who uses the clouds as a footstool for His feet. Sometimes we need to take the time to read passages like the one in Isaiah to remember our thrice holy God, the One who is worthy of our worship and praise. We need to marvel in wonder and amazement at our holy God. In the process, it reminds us who we are as creatures made to worship.

The Fall and Our Worship

So what happened? We know we were created to worship God. We were made to glorify and enjoy Him. We were made to reflect Him in all that we do. That is our purpose in life. Why don't we?

When God created our first parents, Adam and Eve, they worshipped Him and gave Him the honor He deserved. They did all for His glory: their work in the Garden glorified Him. Their rest from labor glorified Him. Their relationship with each other glorified Him. They found their joy and happiness in Him. They were fully known by Him. They enjoyed being in His presence.

But then one day, Satan came and tempted Eve. He said, 'Did God actually say, "You shall not eat of any tree in the garden"?' (Gen. 3:1). He twisted the truth for there was only one tree from which they were forbidden to eat (Gen. 2:16-17). Eve then responded with more twisted truth, 'We may eat of the fruit of the trees in the garden, but God said, "You shall not eat of the fruit of the tree that is in the midst of the garden, neither shall you touch it, lest you die"' (Gen. 3:2-3). (God did not forbid them from touching the tree.)

Satan enticed her with the promise of being like God and the rest is history. '"For God knows that when you eat of it your eyes will be opened, and you will be like God, knowing good and evil." So when the woman saw that the tree was good for food, and that it was a delight to the eyes, and that the tree was to be desired to make one wise, she took of its fruit and ate, and she also gave some to her husband who was with her, and he ate. Then the eyes of both were opened, and they knew that they were naked. And they sewed fig leaves together and made themselves loincloths' (Gen. 3:5-7).

Sin then entered the world and, as a result, we don't give God the glory He is due. We don't enjoy knowing Him and being known by Him. Instead, we desire all the glory for ourselves for we too, like our parents before us, want to be like God. 'And man, as originally created, was a true image of God because he was God-centered rather than self-centered. His one thought and desire, before sin ruined everything, was to serve God and to take delight in Him. When man (Adam) first sinned against God all was changed. Instead of thinking about how great and wonderful God is, he began to think about himself. He began to think of what it would be like if he (Adam) himself could be great, and of how he could enjoy himself!'[7]

Worship Anything

After the Fall, mankind still worshipped, but instead of worshipping the one true God, we worship anything and everything else. We seek after our own glory. We seek after things we think will make us happy, whole, and complete. We seek after false substitute gods and give them the honor that God alone deserves.

Paul tells us in Romans 1 what happened:

> For the wrath of God is revealed from heaven against all ungodliness and unrighteousness of men, who by their unrighteousness suppress the truth. For what can be known about God is plain to them, because God has shown it to them. For his invisible attributes, namely, his eternal power and divine nature, have been clearly perceived, ever since the creation of the world, in the things that have been made. So they are without excuse. For although they knew God, they did not honor him as God or give thanks to him, but they became futile in their thinking, and their foolish hearts were darkened.

7. Williamson, G.I., p.1.

Claiming to be wise, they became fools, and exchanged the glory of the immortal God for images resembling mortal man and birds and animals and creeping things. Therefore God gave them up in the lusts of their hearts to impurity, to the dishonoring of their bodies among themselves, because they exchanged the truth about God for a lie and worshiped and served the creature rather than the Creator, who is blessed forever! Amen (Rom. 1:18-25).

We have all sinned and fall short of the glory of God (Rom. 3:23). In our sin, we suppress the truth about who God is (Rom. 1:18). God's power and holiness is plain in all that He has made (Rom. 1:19-20). Though humanity knows God exists and knows that He is all powerful, humans are foolish and reject God. They turn to worship things created instead of worshipping the Creator. When humans reject God and worship false gods, God 'gives them up' to follow the lusts of their heart (Rom. 1:24). 'In every instance the giving up to sin is a result of idolatry, the refusal to make God the center and circumference of all existence, so that in practice the creature is exalted over the Creator. Hence, all individual sins are a consequence of the failure to prize and praise God as the giver of every good thing.'[8]

A good example of someone living for the lusts of their heart and worshipping things created is St Augustine. Before coming to faith in Christ, he lived a wild life. Some might say he was a playboy. He described his adolescence, 'For I even burnt in my youth, heretofore, to be satiated in things below; and I dared to grow wild again, with these

---

8. *ESV Study Bible* (Wheaton, IL: Crossway, 2008), Kindle location: 291547.

various and shadowy loves: my beauty consumed away, and I stank in Thine eyes; pleasing myself, and desirous to please in the eyes of men.'[9]

He feasted on the idols of life: sex, alcohol, knowledge, laziness, and even thievery. He had a child with a concubine with whom he lived until his mother found a wife for him. 'For it was my sin, that not in Him, but in His creatures—myself and others—I sought for pleasures, sublimities, truths, and so fell headlong into sorrows, confusions, errors.'[10] He even tried various religions and followed different philosophies, but still felt restless, lost, and miserable.

One of Augustine's most famous quotes is 'Thou madest us for Thyself, and our heart is restless, until it repose in Thee.'[11] *Confessions* is his biography describing that journey of restless wandering until he finally found rest in Christ. More than a biography, it is actually a prayer from him to God. In it, he confesses his sin. He asks God difficult questions about life. He voices his longing to love God more and the reason he confessed his sins in such detail, 'For love of Thy love I do it; reviewing my most wicked ways in the very bitterness of my remembrance, that Thou mayest grow sweet unto me.'[12]

After exploring different philosophies of thought, Augustine met the Bishop Ambrose who answered his many

---

9. St. Augustine, *The Confessions of St. Augustine* (New York, NY: Barnes and Noble, 2003), p. 22.

10. Ibid., p. 21.

11. Ibid., p. 1.

12. Ibid., p. 22.

questions about the Bible. Sometime after that encounter, he turned to the book of Romans and read, 'Let us walk properly as in the daytime, not in orgies and drunkenness, not in sexual immorality and sensuality, not in quarreling and jealousy. But put on the Lord Jesus Christ, and make no provision for the flesh, to gratify its desires' (Rom. 13:13-14). He then came to faith and was baptized.

As one who knew well what life was like worshipping created things rather than the Creator, Augustine gives us encouragement in our journey, 'O crooked paths! Woe to the audacious soul, which hoped, by forsaking Thee, to gain some better thing! Turned it hath, and turned again, upon back, sides, and belly, yet all was painful, and Thou alone rest. And behold, Thou art at hand, and deliverest us from our wretched wanderings, and placest us in Thy way, and dost comfort us, and say, "Run; I will carry you; yea I will bring you through; there also will I carry you."'[13]

A Return to Worship

As Augustine noted, God delivers us from ourselves. Though our worship was broken in the Fall, though our sin nature causes us to worship created things rather than the Creator, God made a way to redeem our hearts back to Him, our first love—through the death of His Son.

R.C. Sproul wrote, 'Loving a holy God is beyond our moral power. The only kind of God we can love by our sinful nature is an unholy god, an idol made by our own hands. Unless we are born of the Spirit of God, unless God sheds His holy love in our hearts, unless He stoops

---

13.Ibid., p. 119.

in His grace to change our hearts, we will not love Him…
To love a holy God requires grace, grace strong enough
to pierce our hardened hearts and awaken our moribund
souls.'[14]

At just the right time, God sent His Son as the Second
Adam, wrapped in human skin and bones, to live the life
we could not live. Fully God and fully man, Jesus Christ
lived in this fallen world. He experienced the brokenness
of life in this world: He lived in poverty; He knew loss and
grief; He knew hunger; He knew rejection, temptation,
and fear. Yet He never sinned. Jesus perfectly fulfilled the
law on our behalf. Through faith in what He has done, we
are united to Him, adopted into the family of God, and
made new.

In Christ, we have been given new life through 'the
power of God, who saved us and called us to a holy calling, not because of our works but because of his own purpose and grace, which he gave us in Christ Jesus before the
ages began, and which now has been manifested through
the appearing of our Savior Christ Jesus, who abolished
death and brought life and immortality to light through
the gospel' (2 Tim. 1:8-10). The gospel tells us that because of Christ, we are redeemed from sin and purified
to live for Him. We are being remade into worshippers
who worship in spirit and truth. If you are in Christ, this
is good news! We don't have to worship lesser gods and
created things. We have been set free from slavery to sin
and are now free to worship God. 'For our sake he made

---

14. Sproul, R.C., p.180.

him to be sin who knew no sin, so that in him we might become the righteousness of God' (2 Cor. 5:21).

This means that when God looks upon us, He sees Christ's perfect life lived for us. He sees Christ's righteousness and His life lived to the glory of the Father. He sees Jesus in the temple, praising and worshipping Him. He sees Jesus standing firm against temptation. He sees Jesus' obedient life—from birth to His final breath. He sees Jesus eating, serving, working, teaching, loving, resting, worshipping, and doing all things to the glory of God. Every moment of our Savior's life is credited to us as if we had done it ourselves.

When Jesus ascended into heaven, He sent His Spirit to live in the hearts of believers. 'But the Helper, the Holy Spirit, whom the Father will send in my name, he will teach you all things and bring to your remembrance all that I have said to you' (John 14:26). The Holy Spirit has made a home within us. He comforts us, guides us, convicts us, instructs us, and prays for us. The Spirit enables and empowers us to worship and glorify God. Though we are tempted and often give in to the desire to worship lesser things, we are strengthened by the work of the Spirit in us to put to death our idolatrous worship and learn to live more and more for God's glory alone.

As I mentioned earlier, the process of growth in sanctification involves a 'putting off' and a 'putting on.' Because of what Christ has done for us, we are new creations. God sees us as new in our positional sanctification. We also have to live out that newness in our progressive sanctification. The Apostle Paul instructed the church in Colossians 3, 'If then you have been raised with Christ, seek the things that are above, where Christ is, seated at the right hand of God. Set your minds on things that are above, not on things that are on earth. For you have died, and your life is hidden with Christ in God' (vv. 1-3). Because we are in Christ, we have died to our old self, the self that was enslaved by sin. In Christ, we have risen to new life. Therefore, we are to seek the things of Christ. In essence, Paul says, 'If you are a believer in Christ, you have been changed. What Christ did in his life, death, and resurrection happened to you as well. You are new. So seek after Christ.'

Paul continued, teaching them to 'put off' the old self and 'put on' the new self. 'Put to death therefore what is earthly in you: sexual immorality, impurity, passion, evil desire, and covetousness, which is idolatry ... But now you must put them all away: anger, wrath, malice, slander, and obscene talk from your mouth. Do not lie to one another, seeing that you have put off the old self with its practices and have put on the new self, which is being renewed in knowledge after the image of its creator' (Col. 3:5, 8-10). We are to 'put off' the sin of our old self and 'put on' our new self, the one that is being sanctified and transformed into the image of Christ.

Remember, the process of sanctification is the work of the Spirit of God in us, but also one in which we participate. We are to actively pursue growth in holiness. Just like our toddlers change their clothes multiple times a day, we are to spend our days 'putting off' our old self and 'putting on' our new self. As we recognize and identify sin in our lives, we put it to death, remembering that we are new creations, raised to life in Christ. We are to live out the truth of what we *already are* in Christ.

Moms, Christ has made it possible for us to return to the worship we were created to do. As we talk about idolatry in our lives, we will have to rest and rely upon this gospel truth for apart from Christ, we can do nothing.

Questions for a Mother's Heart:

1. What does it mean to you that you were made to worship, glorify, and enjoy God?

2. Read Psalm 42:1-2. Has your soul ever felt this way?

3. Read Psalm 27:4. What is the one thing David desires?

4. Read Luke 10:38-42. Jesus also references 'one thing.' What is it? Can you see how she is both glorifying and enjoying Him?

5. Consider Augustine's quote from above: 'For love of Thy love I do it; reviewing my most wicked ways in the very bitterness of my remembrance, that Thou mayest grow sweet unto me.' As we evaluate our own hearts and consider the idols we embrace, may that be our purpose as well: for the love of God, that He would grow sweet to us.

A Prayer for a Mother's Heart:

Dear Father,

Thank you for creating me. Thank you for making me your own. As I consider what you made me to be, I realize how far I fall short. I am a worshipper but too often, I worship what you've created rather than you, the Maker and Sustainer of all things.

You alone are worthy of my worship. You alone are God. You rule all things and by your grace I have life, breath, and everything else. Forgive me for failing to worship you as you deserve. Forgive me for not glorifying you in all that I say and do. Forgive me for not shining as a light in this dark world so that others might know who you are.

Help me as I look at idolatry in my life. Open the spiritual eyes of my heart that I might see the idols I've placed on the throne of my heart. Help me to grieve this idolatry and turn from it.

Thank you for Christ, whose death covers my false worship, whose righteousness makes perfectly acceptable my imperfect worship, and whose power enables me to worship in a way that pleases you.

It's because of Jesus and what He's done for me that I can pray, and in His name I cry out to you,

Amen.

3

WHAT IS IDOLATRY?

Buddha. Money. Happiness. Brahma. Sex. Personal Fulfill-
ment. Respect. Family. These are all idols. Some are tangible,
things we can see and hold, others are not. Some are carved
images people bow down to and worship; others are idols
that rule the throne of our hearts.

In the West, we don't often see the idol worship of those
in the East. If we were to visit a country like Nepal, we
would see the prayer flags flying, supposedly carrying the
people's prayers in the wind. If we took a trip to India,
we might see people bathing in the sacred Ganges River,
in the hopes it would wash away their sins. If we were
to travel north of India to various provinces of China,
we would come across Buddhist monasteries where the

monks spend their life in prayer, meditation, and study, hoping that a life of discipline and asceticism will allow them to gain enough merits in this life to reach nirvana in the afterlife. In other places in Asia, we might meet people who practice Taoism, which includes the practice of ancestor worship.

While the idols of our lives in the West are not made of wood, stone, or metal, they exist nonetheless. Though we might not bring offerings to a statue, bathe in a sacred river, or worship our ancestors, we have our own false gods we worship. Tim Keller defines an idol as 'anything more important to you than God, anything that absorbs your heart and imagination more than God, anything you seek to give you what only God can give. A counterfeit god is anything so central and essential to your life that, should you lose it, your life would feel hardly worth living. An idol has such a controlling position in your heart that you can spend most of your passion and energy, your emotional and financial resources, on it without a second thought.'[1] Such idols might include but are not limited to: success, relationships, power, money, education, health, and beauty. All idols are things we look to for comfort, hope, peace, life, worth, and salvation—all things only God can provide.

In this chapter, we will build a foundation by looking deeper at the meaning of idolatry. This will prepare us before we move into looking at specific idols of a mother's heart.

---

1. Keller, Timothy, *Counterfeit Gods: The Empty Promises of Money, Sex, and Power, and the Only Hope that Matters* (New York, NY: Dutton, 2009), pp. xvii-xviii.

At Mount Sinai

You may remember that God's people spent some time in Egypt. They originally came there as refugees of sorts during a famine. Over a number of generations, they grew and multiplied as a nation. Pharaoh feared they would rise up against the Egyptians so he enslaved them.

But God heard their cries and rescued and redeemed them from their bondage. He used Moses to lead the people away from Egypt, opening a path through the sea for them to cross over to the other side. Once they stepped onto the dry land, they rejoiced and praised God, singing and dancing for joy at their rescue. For a time, they didn't know if they would make it. Pharaoh and his army seemed to have the upper hand as they pursued them with vengeance. They thought for sure he would catch up to them. But they didn't know their God and what He could do.

The Israelites didn't know what God could do because they had spent 400 years in slavery. All they knew was life in Egypt where idol worship was rampant. The Egyptians had a god for everything. In fact, they had more gods and goddesses than we could count. These gods had a human body and the head of an animal. There was the god of the scribes, the god of the dead, the god of power, and the god of the sun. Even individual towns had their own god. It was this culture and this home that the Israelites left to follow after the one true God.

God brought them through the desert, providing them water from a rock and bread that appeared on the ground six mornings a week. He led them to Mt Sinai where He proceeded to instruct them in what it looked like to be His people. He taught them what it meant to be set apart from the nations. Moses went to the top of the mountain to receive the Ten Commandments while the people stayed down in camp below. From the bottom of Mt Sinai, they heard loud thunder booming from above. The mountain shook; they were terrified. And rightfully so. In fact, they were instructed to not even touch the mountain because if they did so, they would die (Exod. 19:12-13).

The first commandment God gave Moses was 'You shall have no other gods before me.' The second was, 'You shall not make for yourself a carved image, or any likeness of anything that is in heaven above, or that is in the earth beneath, or that is in the water under the earth. You shall not bow down to them or serve them, for I the LORD your God am a jealous God, visiting the iniquity of the fathers on the children to the third and fourth generation of those who hate me, but showing steadfast love to thousands of those who love me and keep my commandments' (Exod. 20:3-6). The third commandment was to revere God's name and not use it in vain. And the fourth commandment was to remember the Sabbath day and keep it holy. The first four of the Ten Commandments have to do with how God's people worship and honor God.

Moses read them God's law and then returned to speak to God on the mountain. Moses was gone for a long time because God was giving him all the rules they needed to know in order to live as His people in the land to which they were headed. He also gave Moses instructions for how to construct the tabernacle and what to put in it. The Israelites grew concerned. What if Moses didn't return? What if he died up there? Then what would they do? They were quick to forget the amazing things that took place during the plagues in Egypt, the crossing of the Red Sea, the death of all who chased after them, and God's provisions to them thus far in their journey.

They came to Aaron and said, 'Up, make us gods who shall go before us. As for this Moses, the man who brought us up out of the land of Egypt, we do not know what has become of him' (Exod. 32:1). Aaron told them to give him the gold jewelry they wore. (Ironically, God provided the Israelites with plunder from the Egyptians before they left, including gold jewelry: see Exod. 3:22.) Aaron then fashioned a golden calf out of the gold and said, 'These are your gods, O Israel, who brought you up out of the land of Egypt!' (v. 4). They then offered burnt offerings.

Israel did exactly what God had forbidden, what He had just scratched into the stone tablets on the mountain. God, knowing what they were doing, said to Moses, 'Go down, for your people, whom you brought up out of the land of Egypt, have corrupted themselves. They have turned aside quickly out of the way that I commanded them. They have made for themselves a golden calf and have worshiped it and sacrificed to it' (Exod. 32:7-8).

It might seem strange to us in our modern day for someone to craft an idol to bow down to and worship. It's easy to look at the Israelites' sin of idolatry and be amazed at how forgetful they were about all God had done in their life to rescue them. We might remark at how quickly they disregarded God's commands. But in truth, we are just as forgetful and just as disregarding. With our own idols, we forget who God is and what He has done for us. We too turn to false gods in worship, violating God's commands.

Often, in our own seasons of waiting on God, we turn to idols to give us hope, comfort, and peace.

When we worry and fear the future, rather than turning to God for help, we often bow down to the idol of control and seek to manage the things we fear. We do the same thing when we worship money: instead of turning to God in gratitude for what He has provided, we rely on ourselves. We sacrifice our lives and relationships for the sake of earning more; we depend upon money to buy us things to make us happy. We also lack generosity, clinging tightly to what we have instead of sharing with others. Rather than find the love we need in Christ, we worship relationships and the esteem and affirmation we receive from them. We might manage and manipulate those relationships to give us what we think we need from them. We depend upon them for love and affection and when they let us down, we find ourselves filled with despair.

An idol is truly anything we worship apart from God. As Paul Tripp wrote, 'Human beings by their very nature are worshippers. Worship is not something we do; it defines who we are. You cannot divide human beings into those who worship and those who don't. Everybody worships; it's just a matter of what, or whom, we serve.'[2]

After the Israelites crafted a golden calf and worshipped it, God sent Moses down from Sinai to deal with them. God burned in anger against the Israelites for their sin. He told Moses that He would destroy them (Exod. 32:9-10).

---

2. Tripp, Paul, *Instruments in the Redeemer's Hands: People in Need of Change Helping People in Need of Ch*ange (Phillipsburg, NJ: P&R Publishing, 2002), p. 44.

Moses stepped in and mediated for the people. He asked God to relent.

> O LORD, why does your wrath burn hot against your people, whom you have brought out of the land of Egypt with great power and with a mighty hand? ... Remember Abraham, Isaac and Israel, your servants, to whom you swore by your own self, and said to them, 'I will multiply your offspring as the stars of heaven, and all this land that I have promised I will give to your offspring, and they shall inherit it forever.' (Exod. 32:11, 13).

God relented. Moses foreshadowed what Christ would eventually come to do: make peace for us with God.

Law or Grace?

At this point, you may be thinking, 'Why all this business about the Ten Commandments? We aren't under the law, but under grace.' It's true, we are under grace. The Apostle Paul wrote that the law served to show us our need for grace. Without the law, we wouldn't know our sinfulness and wouldn't see our need for a perfect law keeper.

> Why then the law? It was added because of transgressions, until the offspring should come to whom the promise had been made, and it was put in place through angels by an intermediary. Now an intermediary implies more than one, but God is one. Is the law then contrary to the promises of God? Certainly not! For if a law had been given that could give life, then righteousness would indeed be by the law. But the Scripture imprisoned everything under sin, so that the promise by faith in Jesus Christ might be given to those who believe. Now before faith came, we were held captive under the law,

imprisoned until the coming faith would be revealed. So then, the law was our guardian until Christ came, in order that we might be justified by faith. But now that faith has come, we are no longer under a guardian, for in Christ Jesus you are all sons of God, through faith (Gal. 3:19-26).

When we say that we are not under the law, it means that we are not saved by keeping the law. God knew we couldn't keep the law even when He etched it onto stone at Mt Sinai. Moses foretold in Deuteronomy 31:29 that the Israelites would break the law. Despite that, the law served a purpose: to tell us what God required, to teach us about who God is, to point out sin, and to reveal our need for Christ.

Because the Promised One has come, we are now under grace: we are saved by grace through faith in Jesus. As Martin Luther argued in his book, *The Bondage of the Will*, 'the effect, the work, and the office of the law, is to be a light to the ignorant and the blind; such a light, as discovers to them disease, sin, evil, death, hell, and the wrath of God; though it does not deliver from these, but shews them only. And when a man is thus brought to a knowledge of the disease of sin, he is cast down, is afflicted, nay despairs: the law does not help him, much less can he help himself. Another light is necessary, which might discover to him the remedy. This is the voice of the Gospel, revealing Christ as the Deliverer from all these evils.'[3]

---

3. Luther, Martin, *The Bondage of the Will* (Greensboro, NC: Legacy Publications, 2011), Kindle Location: 3728.

Because we are saved by grace and not by keeping the law, does that then mean we can disregard God's commands? Does it mean that obeying God doesn't matter? No. Paul wrote in Romans: 'What then? Are we to sin because we are not under law but under grace? By no means!' (Rom. 6:15). In fact, to continue in sin is to deny what Christ has done for us. 'How can we who died to sin still live in it? Do you not know that all of us who have been baptized into Christ Jesus were baptized into his death? We were buried therefore with him by baptism into death, in order that, just as Christ was raised from the dead by the glory of the Father, we too might walk in newness of life' (Rom. 6:2-4).

So when it comes to the Ten Commandments and what they have to do with us as believers today, they stand as God's instruction for us in what it looks like to honor and obey Him. We know we are sinners who fail to obey Him perfectly. But we have a great Savior who obeyed the law perfectly for us. This is why the gospel is so important. We don't just repent and believe when we first come to faith; we must repent and apply the gospel to our life each and every day. We have to constantly, moment by moment, turn to the gospel and appropriate what Christ did for us. When we fail to love God with all our heart, we have to confess our sin and turn from it, trusting in Christ as our mediator. When we realize we are worshipping an idol, we must confess and repent. Rinse and repeat, as they say. This is the life of a Christian.

We who are in Christ are united to Him. We have died to sin and now live in righteousness—Christ's righteousness. As a result, we are no longer enslaved to our sin. This means we have been set free to obey Him. Through the Spirit at work in us, we can grow in our love for God. We can turn from worshipping things created to the One who created all things. 'So you also must consider yourselves dead to sin and alive to God in Christ Jesus. Let not sin therefore reign in your mortal body, to make you obey its passions. Do not present your members to sin as instruments for unrighteousness, but present yourselves to God as those who have been brought from death to life, and your members to God as instruments for righteousness. For sin will have no dominion over you, since you are not under law but under grace' (Rom. 6:11-14).

What this means is, idolatry doesn't have the final say, the gospel does.

A Matter of the Heart

While much of the idolatry mentioned in the Bible is of actual images crafted from wood or stone, in the book of Ezekiel, God said that the elders of Israel placed idols on the throne of their hearts, 'Son of man, these men have taken their idols into their hearts, and set the stumbling block of their iniquity before their faces' (Ezek. 14:3). The Bible often refers to 'the heart' of man. Before we go too much further, it's important to understand what that term means. When the Bible talks about the human heart, it doesn't mean our real heart—the one that beats in our chest and keeps our body alive. It also isn't referring to the heart shaped candies or chocolates we give those we love on Valentine's Day. The Bible uses the term 'heart' to mean our inner self, who we are as a person, our identity. The real us.

This inner self includes our thoughts, our desires, our feelings, our personality, our motives and intentions, and the choices we make. 'As in water face reflects face, so the heart of man reflects the man' (Prov. 27:19). 'Keep your heart with all vigilance, for from it flow the springs of life' (Prov. 4:23). *What we worship, we worship in our heart.*

Because we are sinners, our hearts are prone to sin. What we need is a new heart. God promised this in the book of Ezekiel: 'And I will give them one heart, and a new spirit I will put within them. I will remove the heart of stone from their flesh and give them a heart of flesh, that they may walk in my statutes and keep my rules and obey them. And they shall be my people, and I will be their God' (Ezek. 11:19-20). This is what the Spirit does in us when He awakens our dead heart to life. He gives us a new heart, a heart capable of responding to God in faith and living to love and obey God. Theologians call this awakening 'regeneration.' 'But God, being rich in mercy, because of the great love with which he loved us, even when we were dead in our trespasses, made us alive together with Christ' (Eph. 2:4-5).

The Throne of Our Heart

In Mark 12, a scribe asked Jesus what the greatest commandment was. Jesus answered, 'The most important is, "Hear, O Israel: The Lord our God, the Lord is one. And you shall love the Lord your God with all your heart and with all your soul and with all your mind and with all your strength." The second is this: "You shall love your neighbor as yourself." There is no other commandment greater than these' (vv. 29-31). Jesus told the scribe to love God with all that he is, not just outwardly in his actions and behaviors, but also inwardly with his whole heart. He also summed up the Ten Commandments in these two statements. The first half of the law has to do with love for God, the other half with love for neighbor.

In Matthew 19, a rich young man came to Jesus. He asked,

> 'Teacher, what good deed must I do to have eternal life?' And he said to him, 'Why do you ask me about what is good? There is only one who is good. If you would enter life, keep the commandments.' He said to him, 'Which ones?' And Jesus said, 'You shall not murder, You shall not commit adultery, You shall not steal, You shall not bear false witness, Honor your father and mother, and, You shall love your neighbor as yourself.' The young man said to him, 'All these I have kept. What do I still lack?' Jesus said to him, 'If you would be perfect, go, sell what you possess and give to the poor, and you will have treasure in heaven; and come, follow me.' When the young man heard this he went away sorrowful, for he had great possessions (Matt. 19: 16-22).

In response to the young man's question, Jesus listed the commands at the latter half of the Ten Commandments. He left out the commandments having to do with love for God. Though the young man had shown righteousness by his outward behavior toward others, inwardly he was not devoted to God. He didn't love God with all his heart; he loved his riches more. That's why when Jesus told him to sell everything he owned and follow Him, he couldn't. His love for his riches was his idol.

Elsewhere in Scripture, Jesus said, 'No servant can serve two masters, for either he will hate the one and love the other, or he will be devoted to the one and despise the other. You cannot serve God and money' (Luke 16:13). The rich young man couldn't love God and love his riches. Likewise, we can't love and serve God and love and serve something else. It's either one or the other. As Kyle Idleman wrote, 'When we hear God say, "You will have no other gods before me," we think of it as a hierarchy: God is always in first place. But there are no places. God isn't interested in competing against others or being first among many. God will not be a part of any hierarchy … He is God, and there are no other applicants for that position. There are no partial gods, no honorary gods, no interim gods, no assistants to the regional gods.'[4]

This is the kind of idolatry in which Christians participate. While the unregenerate (or non-believers) have no love for God and all their affections are for false gods, as believers we love and worship God by grace through faith; we trust in what Christ has done for us at the cross. But we put God in a hierarchy. We often worship God *plus* something else. We put our hope and trust in God *plus* a better job. We seek after God *plus* a fulfilling relationship. We find our meaning in God *plus* motherhood. But God alone is the one true God. He will not share the throne of our heart with anything or anyone else.

As we look at the idols of motherhood, we will be considering those things we add to our worship of God—

---

4. Idleman, Kyle, *Gods at War: Defeating the Idols that Battle for Your Heart* (Grand Rapids, MI: Zondervan, 2013), p. 23.

those things we put our hope and trust in *plus* our love and worship of God.

Idolatry is Adultery

Why won't God share the throne of our heart with anything else? Because idolatry is adultery. The Bible often compares idolatry to adultery. Adultery is when a husband or wife cheats on their spouse with someone else. They are in a covenant relationship, a commitment, with their spouse. By cheating, they are breaking that commitment.

God refers to Himself as our Husband. 'For your Maker is your husband, the LORD of hosts is his name; and the Holy One of Israel is your Redeemer, the God of the whole earth he is called' (Isa. 54:5). Like a jealous husband whose wife had an affair, God is jealous for our hearts. In fact, that is one of the names He calls Himself, 'for you shall worship no other god, for the LORD, whose name is Jealous, is a jealous God' (Exod. 34:14). When God's people turn to worship idols, they are breaking their covenant with Him, just as an unfaithful spouse breaks their covenant when they commit adultery. 'And the LORD said to Moses, "Behold, you are about to lie down with your fathers. Then this people will rise and whore after the foreign gods among them in the land that they are entering, and they will forsake me and break my covenant that I have made with them"' (Deut. 31:16). Indeed God's response and description of Israel's idolatry sounds like that of a spouse, '... how I have been broken over their whoring heart that has departed from me and over their eyes that go whoring after their idols' (Ezek. 6:9).

In the book of Hosea, God called the prophet to marry a prostitute, Gomer (Hosea 1:2). His marriage was a parable in which he lived out what Israel was doing to God in their adultery with other gods. Hosea's marriage paralleled Israel's relationship to God. Even Hosea's children were given names representing God's punishment for Israel (see Hosea 1:4, 6, 8). This parallel is seen most vividly in this passage: 'And the Lord said to me, "Go again, love a woman who is loved by another man and is an adulteress, even as the LORD loves the children of Israel, though they turn to other gods and love cakes of raisins." So I bought her for fifteen shekels of silver and a homer and a lethech of barley' (Hosea 3:1-2).

God told Hosea that He would punish Israel for her idolatry, 'Now I will uncover her lewdness in the sight of her lovers, and no one shall rescue her out of my hand ... And I will punish her for the feast days of the Baals when she burned offerings to them and adorned herself with her ring and jewelry, and went after her lovers and forgot me, declares the Lord' (Hosea 2:10,13). He did so by sending her off into exile.

God prophesied of a day coming when He would extend His mercy and grace to Israel. 'And in that day, declares the LORD, you will call me "My Husband," and no longer will you call me "My Baal." For I will remove the names of the Baals from her mouth, and they shall be remembered by name no more ... And I will betroth you to me forever. I will betroth you to me in righteousness and in justice, in steadfast love and mercy. I will betroth you to me in faithfulness. And you shall know the LORD' (Hosea 2:16-17, 19-20). This day has come in the person and work of Jesus Christ. He ransomed and redeemed His Bride, the church. He set us free from our bondage and slavery to idols. He united us to Him by faith, like a bride to her husband. And one day we will see our Bridegroom face to face, 'Let us rejoice and exult and give him the glory, for the marriage of the Lamb has come, and his Bride has made herself ready' (Rev. 19:7).

Relationship between Sin and Idolatry

I love old things; I collect old, vintage, and antique things. I often imagine the people who might have used an item, what they used the item for, and what their life was like in the past.

A number of years ago, on one of my trips to an antique shop, I found an old window. It was out back, behind the shop in a pile of old windows. The window was covered in orange and black spray paint. There were layers and layers of paint on it. I guess that's why I was able to buy the window for only five dollars!

I took it home and began the process of removing all the layers of paint. It was a laborious process, stripping off each layer, one by one. But when I got to the end, I could finally see the original color of the window. Today it hangs on the wall in my house, a reminder of what often lies hidden beneath the layers of life.

When we look at the sin in our lives, those sins are just at the top layer, like the layers of paint on my window. When we look beneath those sins, we'll see the sin at their core: idolatry.

R.C. Sproul wrote in *The Holiness of God*, 'Sin is cosmic treason. Sin is treason against a perfectly pure Sovereign. It is an act of supreme ingratitude toward the One to whom we owe everything, to the One who has given us life itself.'[5] When we consider the sins we commit, they are all sins against God. Even the ones we commit against others. That is why when David sinned against Bathsheba and Uriah, he confessed to God, 'Against you, you only, have I sinned and done what is evil in your sight, so that you may be justified in your words and blameless in your judgment' (Ps. 51:4).

Our sins are acts of defiance against our Creator. They are statements to God and the world around us, saying, 'I know better. I can do what I want. God can't tell me what to do.' Like the first sin in the Garden, we want to be like God. When we sin, we make a claim that God is not God; rather, we are. In that moment, we are not honoring God as God and instead place ourselves on the throne. Sin defies the first commandment to worship God alone. As Paul Tripp wrote, 'sin is fundamentally idolatrous. I do wrong things because my heart desires something more than the Lord. Sin produces a propensity toward idolatry in us all. We all migrate away from worship and service of the Creator toward worship and service of the created thing. This is the great spiritual war beneath every battle of behavior—the way for control of the heart.' [6]

James helps us see that sin begins in the heart, with our desires. 'Let no one say when he is tempted, "I am being tempted by God," for God cannot be tempted with evil, and he himself tempts no one. But each person is tempted

---

5. Sproul, R.C., *The Holiness of God* (Carol Stream, IL: Tyndale Publishing, 1985), p. 115.

6. Tripp, Paul., p. 66.

when he is lured and enticed by his own desire. Then desire when it has conceived gives birth to sin, and sin when it is fully grown brings forth death' (James 1:13-15). The ungodly desires of our heart give birth to sin. James goes on later to say, 'What causes quarrels and what causes fights among you? Is it not this, that your passions are at war within you? You desire and do not have, so you murder. You covet and cannot obtain, so you fight and quarrel. You do not have, because you do not ask. You ask and do not receive, because you ask wrongly, to spend it on your passions. You adulterous people!' (4:1-4). Sin grows out of our desires for wrong things—things opposed to God and His will. Elise Fitzpatrick notes, 'Our longings and desires are crucial to the study of idolatry because they prompt and channel worship. They are the driving force behind everything we do.'[7]

For example, when we desire to own a home of our own, that's not necessarily a bad thing. We need shelter over our heads to protect us from weather. We need a secure place to sleep where we are safe from those who intend to harm us. Let's say we go house-hunting with a realtor. Perhaps we find a home that is suitable and fits our family's needs. We put in an offer on the house. We are so excited about this home and dream of all that will take place there. We imagine holidays with family and friends. We picture our children growing up there. We plan out how we will decorate it and choose paint colors for all of the rooms.

---

7. Fitzpatrick, Elise M., *Idols of the Heart: Learning to Long for God Alone*, Revised Edition (Phillipsburg, NJ: P&R Publishing, 2016), p. 138.

Then unexpectedly, the deal falls through. We are crushed. It was the home of our dreams and now it is lost. We begin to despair. We think we'll never find a home that beautiful or perfect again. We might even be angry with the homeowners for causing the deal to fall through. That despair and anger reveals that a good desire (a home) became an ungodly desire. The home had become an idol in our heart which we worshipped, thinking it would bring us happiness. We loved the home more than we loved God.

Our idolatry stems from our inordinate desires, our desires that are not for God's glory, but for our own. This idolatry gives birth to sin. While those outside of Christ are enslaved to their desires and cannot do anything but seek after those desires, we who are in Christ have been set free from our old sinful nature. We still have the presence of sin in our lives but the power of sin has been broken through Christ. As the Spirit works in us, transforming us into the likeness of Christ, the more we'll see our sinful desires change. He will show us that Christ alone is all we need; He is the source of our joy, meaning, and happiness. Elise Fitzpatrick provides us some encouragement here, 'He'll work in your heart to enable you to lay down your desires for self-worship and self-love, and He'll place within you the desire to worship and love Him. This will happen as we are assured that His perfect record is ours and we no longer need to seek to save or justify ourselves.[8]

As we move forward, we'll have to do some heart evaluations. We'll have to take a deep look at our longings and desires, our sins and emotional responses, and the idols we

---

8. Ibid., p. 151.

worship. In doing so, may David's prayer be our prayer, 'As a deer pants for flowing streams, so pants my soul for you, O God' (Ps. 42:1).

Questions for a Mother's Heart:

1. Read Proverbs 4:23. What do you think it means to 'guard your heart' (NIV)? How does it relate to idolatry?

2. Why do you think the Bible compares idolatry to adultery?

3. Do you see the relationship between desire and sin?

4. What desires of your heart are competing with a desire for God?

A Prayer for a Mother's Heart:

Father,

I come before you grieved more and more by the ways I do not love you with all my heart. I see now the way my desires give birth to sin. In my sin, I turn from you like a wayward wife turns from her husband to another lover. Each sin is a rejection of you and your place as God.

Through the blood of Christ shed for me, I ask for forgiveness of my idolatry. Forgive me for seeking life in anything else. Forgive me for the sins I've committed in pursuit of my idols. Forgive me for my sinful desires.

I pray that you alone would rule and reign on the throne of my heart. Help me to love you with all my heart, soul, mind, and strength. As the psalmist prayed, 'Create in me a clean heart O God, and renew a right spirit within me' (Ps. 51:10).

In Jesus' name,

Amen.

4

IDENTIFYING IDOLS
IN OUR LIVES

When my kids were young, I had them do a craft project to teach them the concept of idolatry. I talked to them about how we try to fill our hearts with things we think will make us happy. As part of the craft, I had them lay down on a huge sheet of paper and I drew an outline of their body. I then drew a circle shape on the chest of the body. I gave them a pile of magazines and told them to find words and images of things people might love more than God. They were to cut out the images and glue them on the space on the paper.

It was interesting what my kids instinctively recognized as idols. They found images of dollar bills, food, television, phones, and toys and glued them on the paper. I then had them decorate their 'person' however they wanted. They added hair, a face, and clothes. One of them drew on a hat. But the thing that stood out to me most was the frown they added to the face, symbolizing that idols do not bring happiness.

When Idols Fail

As much as we seek happiness in the idols we pursue, they can never give us the joy we find with Christ. The French philosopher, Blaise Pascal, wrote, 'All men seek happiness. This is without exception. Whatever different means they employ, they all tend to this end … What is it then that this desire and this inability proclaim to us, but that there was once in a man a true happiness of which there now remain to him only the mark and empty trace, which he in vain tries to fill from all his surroundings, seeking from things absent the help he does not obtain in things present? But these are all inadequate, because the infinite abyss can only be filled by an infinite and immutable object, that is to say, only by God Himself.'[1]

Some people refer to this 'infinite abyss' as a God-shaped hole. Nothing can fill that space but God Himself. Whatever happiness we do find in our idols is temporary and fleeting. It's like the crash following a sugar rush, or the doldrums of January following the excitement of Christmas. In the end, our idols will fail us. We will feel that restlessness of which Augustine spoke. We will feel a constant dissatisfaction, a lingering discontentment. Until we will realize our idols just can't fill the infinite abyss

---

1. Pascal, Blaise, *Pensées* (New York, NY: Philosophical Library), Kindle Location: 2119, 2126.

in our heart. And until we can see them for what they truly are: counterfeits, false substitutes, cheap imitations, worthless, and powerless.

One of my son's favorite Bible stories comes from 1 Kings 18. In this story, the prophet Elijah challenged the prophets of Baal to see who worshipped the one true God. In doing so, they saw just how weak and powerless their god was. 'And Elijah came near to all the people and said, "How long will you go limping between two different opinions? If the LORD is God, follow him; but if Baal, then follow him"' (v. 21). He gave them a bull to offer in sacrifice to Baal. 'Let two bulls be given to us, and let them choose one bull for themselves and cut it in pieces and lay it on the wood, but put no fire to it. And I will prepare the other bull and lay it on the wood and put no fire to it. And you call upon the name of your god, and I will call upon the name of the LORD, and the God who answers by fire, he is God' (vv. 23-24).

The prophets did all they could to get their god to ignite the sacrifice with fire. They cried out to Baal. They cut themselves. They marched around the altar. But there was no response. 'And at noon Elijah mocked them, saying, "Cry aloud, for he is a god. Either he is musing, or he is relieving himself, or he is on a journey, or perhaps he is asleep and must be awakened"' (v. 27).

So Elijah built an altar to the Lord with a bull as a sacrifice. He poured water over the altar until the wood and sacrifice were saturated. Elijah prayed, 'O LORD, God of Abraham, Isaac, and Israel, let it be known this day that you are God in Israel, and that I am your servant, and that I have done all these things at your word. Answer me,

O LORD, answer me, that this people may know that you, O LORD, are God, and that you have turned their hearts back' (vv. 36-37). Then God consumed the offering with fire. 'And when all the people saw it, they fell on their faces and said, "The LORD, he is God; the LORD, he is God"' (v. 39).

We too need to see the reality of our idols. We need to see their powerlessness. We need to realize God alone is what we need. To begin that process, we need to identify the idols of our hearts.

Even Good Things

As we consider what idolatry is and the idols we worship in our hearts, we might only think of the obvious things that people worship in our culture. Power. Fame. Money. We might look at those who are rich and famous and point out the idols they worship as evidenced by the lifestyle they live. In doing so, we might think that we don't have idols in our own hearts. The truth is, it's not only things like wealth and success that people worship: we can even worship good things. We can worship the things God has given us as blessings in our life: children, marriage, ministry, work, friendships, hobbies, and spiritual gifts. Even, as in the example I gave earlier, sleep can be an idol.

Good things can become bad things when they become the only things that matter in our lives. When we trust in even good things to make our lives better, safer, happier, and more comfortable, they are idols. When we trust in good things to give our lives meaning and purpose, they have become idols. When the good things in our lives control us, direct us, and rule us, they are idols.

When we cling tightly to a dream, a hope, or a goal, and feel as though our lives will lose purpose without those things being fulfilled, they have become idols.

As we discuss idolatry in this book, don't think of idol worship as only worship of bad things. Anything and everything can be an idol. As John Calvin wrote regarding idol worship in the Old Testament, 'man's nature, so to speak, is a perpetual factory of idols.'[2] In our sin nature, we are always searching for idols to worship. And no matter the idol or the motivation behind the worship, when we worship anything apart from God, we are taking from God what is due Him or as Calvin wrote, 'whatever is conferred upon the idol is snatched away from Him.'[3] God is our Maker and Creator, He alone is worthy of worship. When we fail to worship Him as He has called us to, we rob Him of the glory and honor which belong to Him alone.

Identifying Idols

At this point, you may wonder, how do I know what idols I worship? How do I know what I put my hope in apart from God?

When it comes to identifying the idols that reign in our hearts, there are certain questions we can ask ourselves. These are the questions I am going to refer to later when we look at specific idols of motherhood.

---

2. Calvin, John, *Institutes of the Christian Religion*, (Philadelphia: Westminster Press, 1960), p. 108.

3. Ibid., p. 109.

Time and Money

Time and money are our two most valuable assets. How we spend them says a lot about what we value and what is most important to us.

What do you spend your time thinking or daydreaming about? We usually spend a lot of time thinking, planning, and strategizing about our idols. Whatever we value most is what we will spend our time pursuing. We will often sacrifice our time for our idols and find that we have no time for anything else. This often means we don't have time to pray and study God's Word or invest in loving and serving a hurting friend.

Some of us might spend our time making our home perfect in every way—clean, nicely decorated, organized. It's an activity that consumes our time. For others, we might spend our time on our health. Take a look at how you use your time each day—is it in worship of something other than God?

The second area we can look to in determining our idols is where we spend our money. Often what we spend our money on is an indicator of what we love most. And if we don't have the money to buy that thing, how do we respond? Are we angry? Filled with despair? Jesus said, 'Do not lay up for yourselves treasures on earth, where moth and rust destroy and where thieves break in and steal, but lay up for yourselves treasures in heaven, where neither moth nor rust destroys and where thieves do not break in and steal. For where your treasure is, there your heart will be also' (Matt. 6:19-21).

There have been times when I worshipped the affirmation and praise of others. Whether it was in response to the clothes I wore or the way I decorated my home, I enjoyed the response. Spending money on things in order to receive that response was an indicator of idolatry. It meant that I found my meaning and significance in the praise and adoration of others, rather than in what God says about me.

Emotional Responses

Often our strongest emotions are connected to our idols. What are your fears? What keeps you awake at night? What consumes your thoughts? What do you try to protect yourself or your loved ones from?

As moms, we can fear illness and injury in our children. We can fear negative outside influences in their lives. We can fear disorder and chaos in our homes. Whatever it is we fear, we will do whatever it takes to keep that fear from coming true. When you feel fearful this week, take a step back and consider the idol to which it is connected.

Another strong emotion we might experience is anger. What do you get angry about? When our idols are threatened, we can often respond in anger. Consider how angry little children get when another child snatches a toy from them. 'Mine!' they might yell in response. Perhaps someone critiqued your parenting skills and you spent the rest of the day fuming about it. Or maybe your child refused to nap one afternoon, interrupting your time to yourself and you responded in anger. Elise Fitzpatrick notes, 'emotions are mirrors of our hearts. Our emotions reveal our thoughts and intentions; they reveal the judgments we've made about our circumstances.[4]

In Acts 16, Paul and Silas were in Philippi. A demon-possessed slave girl followed Paul around saying, 'These men are servants of the Most High God, who proclaim to you the way of salvation' (Acts 16:17). Paul grew annoyed and commanded the spirit to leave her. When it did, her owners were angry. 'But when her owners saw that their hope of gain was gone, they seized Paul and Silas and dragged them into the marketplace before the rulers ... The crowd joined in attacking them, and the magistrates tore the garments off them and gave orders to beat them with rods. And when they had inflicted many blows upon them, they threw them into prison, ordering the jailer to keep them safely' (vv. 19, 22-23). Likewise, when what we love and worship is attacked, we can also respond in anger.

Control

What controls you? Often the things we worship become the things that rule our lives. Tim Keller wrote, '... whatever we love and trust we also serve. Anything that becomes more important and non-negotiable to us than God becomes an enslaving idol ... Idols control us, since we feel we must have them or life is meaningless.'[5] What are you pulled toward? What defines and rules your days?

---

4. Fitzpatrick, Elise M., *Idols of the Heart: Learning to Long for God Alone*, Revised Edition (Phillipsburg, NJ: P&R Publishing, 2016), p. 222.

5. Keller, Timothy, *Counterfeit Gods: The Empty Promises of Money, Sex, and Power, and the Only Hope that Matters* (New York, NY: Dutton, 2009), p. xxii.

'For whatever overcomes a person, to that he is enslaved' (2 Pet. 2:19).

Idols require sacrifices. In the Old Testament, such sacrifices often involved death. The god Molech was an idol to which parents sacrificed their children (see Lev. 18:21). What or whom have you sacrificed for your idol? Perhaps you have sacrificed relationships with others to satisfy your god. Or maybe you've given up your integrity by lying to keep your idol satisfied. Consider the sacrifices you have made to sustain your idolatry.

Loss

What thing, if you lost it today, would devastate you? What could you not live without? Is it the perfect house or job you've always wanted? Is it respect from others? Is it love and affection? Whatever it is, it acts as a functional savior. It is what you cling to, thinking it makes your life complete. It's also what you protect at all costs. Whatever that thing is, whether it is a material thing, a hope or dream, a relationship, or anything else, if it reigns on the throne of your heart, it is an idol.

In Acts 19, Paul was in Ephesus. A silversmith was there who created silver shrines to the goddess Artemis. He gathered together other craftsmen of idols and said, 'Men, you know that from this business we have our wealth. And you see and hear that not only in Ephesus but in almost all of Asia this Paul has persuaded and turned away a great many people, saying that gods made with hands are not gods. And there is danger not only that this trade of ours may come into disrepute but also that the temple of the great goddess Artemis may be counted as nothing, and that she may even be deposed from her magnificence, she whom all Asia and the world worship' (Acts 19:25-27). This caused a riot. The craftsmen were enraged and they attacked Paul's companions. When we are at risk of losing an idol, this is how the heart responds.

Trust

Where do you place your trust? Martin Luther wrote that an idol, a god, is something 'from which we are to expect all good and to which we are to take refuge in all distress.'[6] An idol is what we place our trust in. It is our refuge, what we turn to for help and hope. In his catechism, Luther wrote that the first commandment teaches that we are to trust in God alone. When we trust in anything else, we worship a false god.

Luther encourages us to evaluate what we trust, 'Ask and examine your heart diligently, and you will find whether it cleaves to God alone or not. If you have a heart that can expect of Him nothing but what is good, especially in want and distress, and that, moreover, renounces and forsakes everything that is not God, then you have the only true God. If, on the contrary, it cleaves to anything else, of which it expects more good and help than of God, and does not take refuge in Him, but in adversity flees from Him, then you have an idol, another god.'[7] Where do you turn to for refuge?

---

6. Luther, Martin, *Small and Large Catechism*, 1529 (Kindle Edition, Location 534).

7. Ibid., Location 600.

If Only

What is your 'if only'? Fill in the blank: if only I had _____ my life would be complete. Our 'if only's say a lot about what's in our heart, what matters the most to us. We look to that thing as the missing piece to make our life whole and complete. We seek after and pursue that thing until we have it.

For many years, my 'if only' was, 'If only my husband worked less, then I would be happy and our family would be happy.' Having a husband home rather than working all the time is certainly a good thing. But for me, it was my 'if only.' It was the one thing I thought would make my life better. And because I didn't have it, I thought it justified my anger and bitterness.

Sin

What sin or sins do you find yourself doing over and over? Remember that our sins are directly related to what we desire. When we sin, we love and worship the wrong thing. We sin to satisfy what we think will fill our longings. Perhaps it is lying and manipulating others to get what you want. Maybe it is chronic worry. Maybe it is sinful lusts and thoughts, the kind that fill you with shame so you keep them hidden and unconfessed. Maybe it is lashing out in anger toward your husband or children. Whatever we worship, whatever we love more than God, we will sin to obtain it.

'Then desire when it has conceived gives birth to sin, and sin when it is fully grown brings forth death' (James 1:15). But there's hope for all of us as sinners, 'Therefore put away all filthiness and rampant wickedness and receive with meekness the implanted word, which is able to save your souls' (James 1:21). Ask yourself, what unmet desire is this sin a response to?

Chaos

What areas of your life seem 'out of control?' Often the places we attempt to control reveal idols. Maybe you spend a lot of time trying to organize your schedule or are strict with your routines. When my children were little, routines were important. They needed their rest. They needed to eat at the same time every day. Such routines were good for them. But I also worshipped those routines. If something or someone interrupted those routines, I responded in frustration. Sometimes even anger. Those routines made life comfortable for me. Schedules and routines may not be the 'out of control' thing in your life. What do you find yourself trying to control and manage?

Barriers

What barriers do you come up against in your life? Often God will put up barriers to keep us from our idols. In the book of Hosea, God described the obstacles He would place in Israel's way to keep her from her idols. 'Therefore I will hedge up her way with thorns, and I will build a wall against her, so that she cannot find her paths. She shall pursue her lovers but not overtake them, and she shall seek them but shall not find them. Then she shall say, "I will go and return to my first husband"' (Hosea 2:6-7).

God will often block the path to our idols. He will keep us from obtaining what we desire. He might leave us empty-handed so that we will turn back to Him. Tim Keller compares this to when Abraham was told to sacrifice Isaac, his only son. He wrote, 'the most painful times in our lives are times in which our Isaacs, our idols, are being threatened or removed … As many have learned and later taught, you don't realize Jesus is all you need until Jesus is all you have.' [8]

Expectations

Another way to identify idols in our lives is to look at our expectations. What do you expect out of life? What do you expect from others, from yourself, from God? Consider your thoughts and beliefs—what are the *'should's* and *'ought-to's'* in your life?

For example, do you believe life should go a certain way? Do you believe people ought to respond to you in a certain way? What do you believe about motherhood? Fill in the blanks: As a mother, I should _____. Or my children should _____. Motherhood ought to be _____.

When our expectations fail us and life doesn't work the way we expect, we often respond in frustration and anger. Or we might internalize that anger so that it grows into despair. Those emotions highlight the fact that what we've placed our hope in has let us down. Take the time to think and pray over your expectations and see what idols are lurking there.

---

8. Keller, Timothy, p. 19.

Feeling Sorry for Ourselves

My pastor once did a series of sermons related to self-pity. He said that the more idolatrous our hearts are, the more we will have self-pity. We feel sorry for ourselves because of some trial, hardship, or injustice and we seek out others who will agree with us, feel sorry for us, and perhaps even intervene on our behalf. [9]

We can see this when our idols fail us, when we don't get what we desire, and when what we desire is taken away from us. Here's an example from the book of 1 Kings:

> Now Naboth the Jezreelite had a vineyard in Jezreel, beside the palace of Ahab king of Samaria. And after this Ahab said to Naboth, 'Give me your vineyard, that I may have it for a vegetable garden, because it is near my house, and I will give you a better vineyard for it; or, if it seems good to you, I will give you its value in money.' But Naboth said to Ahab, 'The LORD forbid that I should give you the inheritance of my fathers.' And Ahab went into his house vexed and sullen because of what Naboth the Jezreelite had said to him, for he had said, 'I will not give you the inheritance of my fathers.' And he lay down on his bed and turned away his face and would eat no food (21:1-4).

Do you see Ahab's response when he didn't get what he wanted? In what ways might you express self-pity?

To review, here are the questions to ask yourself to help in identifying idols in your heart:

---

9. I am thankful to my pastor, Tim Locke, for this insight.

1. What do you spend your time on?

2. What do you spend your money on?

3. What are your strongest emotions? What do you fear? What makes you angry?

4. What controls you?

5. What do you fear losing?

6. What do you trust in to make your life better?

7. What are your 'if-only's?

8. What sin or sins do you constantly battle?

9. What areas of your life seem out of control?

10. What barriers do you face in your life, keeping you from what you want?

11. What do you expect out of life, from yourself, others, and God?

12. What do you feel self-pity about?

Because Jesus was Tempted

In Matthew 4, after He was baptized by the Spirit and honored by the Father, Jesus was led by the Spirit to the wilderness. For forty days He was without food and water. Satan found Him there and tempted Him. Matthew records three specific temptations Jesus endured. First, Satan tempted Jesus to turn stones into bread so that He could eat. Jesus responded, 'It is written, "Man shall not live by bread alone, but by every word that comes from the mouth of God"' (v. 4). Satan tempted Jesus a second time by telling Him to throw Himself from the top of the temple.

Quoting Psalm 91, Satan said that the angels would catch Him. Jesus responded, 'Again it is written: "You shall not put the Lord your God to the test" (v. 7). And last, Satan tempted Jesus by offering Him the kingdoms of the world if He would only bow down and worship him. Jesus said, 'Be gone, Satan! For it is written, "You shall worship the Lord your God and him only shall you serve"' (v. 10).

Each time Satan tempted Him, Jesus responded by countering Satan with God's Word. For most of us, when we've read this passage, we've deduced that it teaches us to counter temptation with God's Word. While it is true that we should defeat lies with the truth (Eph. 6:16), there is more in this passage than simply copying how Jesus responded to Satan.

The passages Jesus quoted were from the book of Deuteronomy. Jesus' forty days in the wilderness remind us of the Israelites' forty years of wilderness wanderings. During those years, they grumbled and complained. They were ungrateful. Even after God had rescued them from slavery and brought them through the sea, they doubted He would provide food and water for them. As we already observed, they worshipped an idol constructed from their gold jewelry. They also refused to obey Moses and Aaron. Moses called them a stiff-necked people.

Jesus' temptation in the wilderness shows us that He is the greater prophet God promised Moses, 'I will raise up for them a prophet like you from among their brothers. And I will put my words in his mouth, and he shall speak to them all that I command him' (Deut. 18:18). Unlike Israel, Jesus perfectly obeyed God. What this passage in Matthew 4 teaches us is that Jesus is the perfect sacrifice for our sins. Because He was tempted and did not sin, He could take our place and bear our sins for us. 'For our sake he made him to be sin who knew no sin, so that in him we might become the righteousness of God' (2 Cor. 5:21).[10]

Our Savior's temptation in the wilderness is good news for those of us who, like the Israelites, are tempted to idolatry. We also turn our back on the One true God and worship created things. We too are quick to forget who God is and what He has done for us. We are quick to grumble and complain. But praise God for Jesus! He is the true Israel, the one who fulfilled what Israel could not do and what *we* cannot do. He is our Savior, Redeemer, Substitute, and Mediator. He is also our help in all our temptations: 'because he himself has suffered when tempted, he is able to help those who are being tempted' (Heb. 2:18). Charles Spurgeon wrote, 'the Lord Jesus, though tempted, gloriously triumphed, and as He overcame, so surely shall His followers also, for Jesus is the representative man for His people; the Head has triumphed, and the members share in the victory … Our place of safety is in the bosom of our Savior.'[11]

Moms, Jesus is your help and hope in each and every moment of the day. Even now, Jesus stands before the Father, interceding on your behalf. He helps you through His Spirit who reminds you of the truth of the gospel and of your redemption from sin. When you face temptation,

---

10. I wrote an article about Jesus' temptation for Christward Collective. You can read it here: http://www.christwardcollective.com/christward/the-tempted-one (accessed May 16, 2018).

11. Spurgeon, Charles, *Morning and Evening* (McLean, VA: MacDonald Publishing, 1973), October 3 devotional.

the Spirit prompts your heart to remember what glorifies God and what does not. He strengthens you to resist giving in to what tempts you. And on those days when you do give in, He helps you confess and repent. In fact, the Spirit is always at work in you, even when you don't feel like anything is happening. He is using every situation in your life to change and transform you.

You can take great hope knowing that you have a Savior who knows what it is to be tempted, who has faced temptation for your sake and won, and who every day is at work helping you face your own temptations. Remember this good news as we move forward in looking at specific idols of a mother's heart.

Questions for a Mother's Heart:

1. Go through the questions in this chapter and prayerfully evaluate them. As you do so, consider the idols you worship.

2. Have your idols ever failed you?

3. What good things do you worship?

4. Read Psalm 115. What happens to people who create and trust in idols? What about those who trust in the Lord?

5. Read Matthew 4:1-11. What does it mean to you that Jesus is the sinless Lamb of God?

A Prayer for a Mother's Heart:

Father in heaven,

As I read through this list, I realize more and more the ways I worship false gods. I see it in my emotional responses, in the ways I spend my time and money, in my thoughts and desires. This list is convicting, Father. But I know that you are at work in me by your Spirit. Though I am crushed now by conviction, I know you will heal me. You will use this to make me more like your Son and for that I am thankful. I pray with the psalmist, 'Purge me with hyssop, and I shall be clean; wash me, and I shall be whiter than snow. Let me hear joy and gladness; let the bones that you have broken rejoice' (Ps. 51:7-8).

Forgive me Father for my sinful thoughts, desires, and emotions. Forgive me for my 'if-only's. Forgive me for my self-pity and for not trusting in you alone. You are my life, my salvation, my hope, my joy. Help me to remember that.

Shower me with your grace today as I face the idols of my heart. May you be glorified in me in this process.

In Jesus' name I pray,

Amen.

PART 2

IDOLS OF A MOTHER'S HEART

5

THE IDOL OF CHILDREN

Like many young girls, as a child I had lots of dolls. I enjoyed changing their clothes, pretending to feed them, and putting them to bed. My mother sewed me dresses for my dolls out of fabric remnants. I had other toys and games I enjoyed playing with as well, but my dolls are ones I still have today. And like other little girls—in addition to being a detective like Nancy Drew—I wanted to be a mom one day.

Motherhood is one of the oldest callings in life. After God created Adam and Eve, they were charged with having children and ruling over the earth, 'And God blessed them. And God said to them, "Be fruitful and multiply and fill the earth and subdue it, and have dominion over the fish of the sea and over the birds of the heavens and over every living thing that moves on the earth'" (Gen. 1:28). Eve's name means 'mother of all living.' As daughters of Eve, being a mother (whether physically, through adoption, or spiritually mothering someone else) is part of what it means for us to live out our womanhood.

The Bible considers children a blessing: 'Behold, children are a heritage from the LORD, the fruit of the womb a reward. Like arrows in the hand of a warrior are the children of one's youth. Blessed is the man who fills his quiver with them! He shall not be put to shame when he speaks with his enemies in the gate' (Ps. 127:3-5). While the disciples wanted to keep little children from coming to Jesus, He instead said, 'Let the little children come to me and do not hinder them, for to such belongs the kingdom of heaven' (Matt. 19:14).

There are a number of stories in the Bible about women desiring to have a child of their own. In 1 Samuel 1, Hannah desired to have a child but the Lord had closed her womb. She prayed to God for a child and promised to give her first-born to Him. She later gave birth to Samuel and brought him to the temple to live and serve the Lord there. 'And in due time Hannah conceived and bore a son, and she called his name Samuel, for she said, "I have asked for him from the LORD"' (1 Sam. 1:20).

Abraham and Sarah were also unable to have children. In their old age, God promised them a child. In fact, He promised that the whole world would be blessed through Abraham's seed. Such a promise was almost too good and too amazing to believe. 'Now Abraham and Sarah were old, advanced in years. The way of women had ceased to be with Sarah. So Sarah laughed to herself, saying, "After I am worn out, and my lord is old, shall I have pleasure?" The LORD said to Abraham, "Why did Sarah laugh and say, 'Shall I indeed bear a child, now that I am old?' Is anything too hard for the LORD? At the appointed time I will return to you, about this time next year, and Sarah shall have a son'" (Gen. 18:11-14). The Lord fulfilled His promise and gave them Isaac.

Ultimately, the promise to bless the world through Abraham's descendants came in the person of Jesus. This child, Jesus, Immanuel, God in the flesh, was the greatest and most longed-for blessing of all. 'She will bear a son, and you shall call his name Jesus, for he will save his people from their sins' (Matt. 1:21).

When Children Become an Idol

Having a child is indeed a wonderful blessing. Being a mother is a blessing. Some would say motherhood is the most important job there is, but like other good things, motherhood becomes a wrong thing when we prize it above God. Yes, it is possible for children to be an idol of our heart. We can place the desire of having a child or the children we have on the altar of our heart and worship them.

Longing for Motherhood

There are multiple ways we can worship children. Being a mother can be an idol itself. Perhaps you've tried to get pregnant and so far have been unsuccessful. Each month that goes by without success makes you more and more anxious. Perhaps you fear you won't be able to get pregnant at all. You've always thought you'd be a mother; now the dream of motherhood feels like it is being snatched away. You may wonder, 'Why, Lord? Why not me?' Perhaps you can relate to Hannah who 'was deeply distressed and prayed to the LORD and wept bitterly' (1 Sam. 1:10). You may look at the growing bellies of friends who are pregnant and struggle not to be bitter at their blessing. You feel empty inside, literally and figuratively.

For some, you may already be a mother. Maybe you have a child but are trying to have a second. You always imagined yourself with two or three children. But it looks like that won't be possible. The picture you had of your family is disappearing before your eyes. You grieve that your only child will grow up without brothers and sisters.

The desire to be a mother is not wrong. It is a good desire. If the dream of motherhood is shattered in some way, it is also a good and right thing to grieve. If you are unable to have a child, if you have lost a child to miscarriage, or lost a child in some other way, it is right and important to grieve such a loss. We should weep and cry out to God as Hannah did. We weep because the loss is real and painful. We grieve because things are not as they should be. Our grief acknowledges that this world is fallen and broken and we feel that brokenness deep within us.

When time has passed and the grief has lessened in intensity, the question becomes: what is your heart's posture? For those who worship motherhood, such a loss lingers long and grows into anger and bitterness. You may find yourself grasping and clinging to the dream, trying to find a way to fill the emptiness inside. You might have looked to that child you wanted as the one thing that would make your life whole and complete. A child was going to give your life the meaning you've desperately needed. Perhaps, like Leah (Gen. 29:32), you thought a baby would change your marriage for the better.

Not everyone who finds themselves without a child necessarily worships the idea of having a child, but some do. It is a question worth talking to the Lord about, asking the Spirit to open your eyes to see the true content of your heart.

Wanting a Redo

Some might desire motherhood for another reason: to somehow make up for a bad childhood. Maybe you come from a broken home. Perhaps your parent or parents were so involved in their own problems and brokenness, they neglected you. Maybe your childhood was so chaotic and frightening you resolved that one day you would have your own family and do it right. You vow to love your child the way you weren't loved. You've promised yourself that you will provide the stable home life you never had. You are going to give your child all that you lacked in love and also in experience, education, toys, sports, and more.

There is nothing wrong with wanting to do the right thing in our motherhood. If we grew up in a violent or chaotic home, it is a good thing to want to do things differently with our own children. We should seek to raise them in a loving and nurturing environment. But the problem comes when we place our hope in that. When we seek a happy home life for our children as a way to make our life better, it has become an idol. We can't make up for the pains of the past by trying to relive them through someone else. Only Christ can heal those pains; only He can redeem our brokenness.

If we seek a redo on life through children, we will only be disappointed. Often, what we find is that we can't control life. We can't manufacture a life. No matter our intentions, sin gets in the way. When we put our hope in making our life a certain way, we are placing our hope in something outside of our control. We are putting our hope in something other than Christ and only He can make us happy and whole.

Living for Our Children

For still others, perhaps you already have children. You know the blessing of having little ones to love and care for. But the problem is, your children have become your everything. You live for them. You live to please them and make them happy. You spend your time thinking of ways to make their life fun and exciting. Whether it's the food they eat, the places they go, the activities they participate in, you work hard to make everything enjoyable for them.

You are active in every area of your children's life. It's almost like they are an extension of yourself. You live through them. This means that what happens to them happens to you. When your child's friend is unkind to them, it's like they are being unkind to you. When a teacher critiques their work, it's like they are critiquing you. When they don't make the sports team, it becomes your failure. Being a mother is what gives you life, meaning, and purpose.

There is a fictional story titled, *Hannah Coulter*, about a woman in old age looking back and telling the story of her life. She talks about her children growing up and moving away from home and how heartbreaking it was for her when that happened. 'After each one of our children went away to the university, there always came a time when we would feel the distance opening to them, pulling them away. It was like sitting snug in the house, and a door is opened somewhere, and suddenly you feel a draft.'[1] My oldest will leave for college in five years. As I read this fictional tale, I couldn't help but think about what my life will be like without my children at home. I wondered, 'Who will I be without someone to take care of?' My days are centered on my children. I cook for them. I teach them. I chauffeur them wherever they need to go. I take care of the details of their lives. What happens to my life when they are out on their own? If my children give my life purpose and meaning, if they are idols in my heart, I will find myself in despair once they are gone. I will feel lost and unanchored.

It's easy for children to become an idol in a mother's heart. We spend so much of our time each day serving them, loving them, teaching and training them—so much so that it's easy to see how our lives can revolve around them. It can be a fine line between doing all the necessary things to care for and raise our children and making all that we do be about them. Idols are tricky in that way. They hide in the shadows so we don't see them clearly. We can think all along that what we are doing is a good and right thing when all the while, we are actually worshipping our children.

There is a good example of this in C.S. Lewis' allegory, *The Great Divorce*, where he weaves a story about a group of people on a bus trip to heaven. He wrote it to

---

1. Berry, Wendell, *Hannah Coulter* (Berkeley, CA: Counterpoint, 2004), p. 120.

explore the reasons why people choose to love and commit themselves to God versus those who choose to live for the things of this world and ultimately, for Hell.

In one chapter, there is a woman named Pam. She is greeted at one of their stops by the departed soul of her brother, who attempts to convince her to journey on to heaven and into the presence of God. She is upset that she wasn't greeted by her dearly loved and departed son, Michael. Her brother explains she isn't ready to see him yet because she must love God first and foremost. She must desire to see God and then she will enjoy the blessings of heaven; not the other way around. 'You're treating God only as a means to Michael. But the whole thickening treatment consists in learning to want God for His own sake.'[2]

In the exchange Pam has with her brother, he points out to her the way she worshipped her son. Pam says, 'I'm sure I did my best to make Michael happy. I gave up my whole life.' Her brother responds, 'Human beings can't make one another really happy for long … He [God] wanted you to love Michael as He understands love. You cannot love a fellow-creature fully till you love God.' Pam later says, 'This is all nonsense—cruel and wicked nonsense. What *right* have you to say things like that about Mother-love? It is the highest and holiest feeling in human nature.' Her brother responds, 'Pam, Pam—no natural feelings are high or low, holy or unholy, in themselves. They are all holy when God's hand is on the rein. They all go bad when they set up on their own and make themselves into false gods.'[3]

---

2. Lewis, C.S., *The Great Divorce* (New York, NY: Macmillan, 1946), pp. 91, 92.

3. Ibid., pp. 94-95.

In this tale, Pam believes that a mother's love is sacred. She believes there is nothing wrong in the love she has for her son. This can be true with us as well. In some ways, worship of our children can be an 'acceptable sin,' one of those sins that everyone does so we often overlook it and accept it. We might think that a good mother invests her life in her children. A good mother devotes herself to her children and sacrifices for them. While motherhood is indeed sacrificial, we must be wary of our heart's tendency to worship good things. Our love for our children must come from the overflow of our love for God.

Like all idols, worshipping our children will let us down. It will fail us. We may find that motherhood doesn't fill us or complete us the way we expect it to. Our children's personalities may be different than what we imagined. Motherhood might be harder than we anticipated. Perhaps we have a child with special needs, an especially challenging child, or a prodigal child. Or we might find ourselves as a single mom, having to bear the burden of parenting all on our own. Perhaps our children are ungrateful for all that we do for them. They may take us for granted. Certainly, our children will come to a stage in their lives where they don't need us all the time; they will want their independence from us. In all of these difficult aspects of motherhood, we'll find the idol of children letting us down. How will we respond? What will we do?

God tested Abraham in Genesis 22 to see if his beloved son, Isaac, was an idol of his heart, 'After these things God tested Abraham and said to him, "Abraham!" And he said, "Here I am." He said, "Take your son, your only son Isaac, whom you love, and go to the land of Moriah, and offer him there as a burnt offering on one of the mountains of which I shall tell you'" (vv. 1-2). Abraham did as God instructed and took Isaac to sacrifice him. 'Then Abraham reached out his hand and took the knife to slaughter his son. But the angel of the LORD called to him from heaven and said, "Abraham, Abraham!" And he said, "Here I am." He said, "Do not lay your hand on the boy or do anything to him, for now I know that you fear God, seeing you have not withheld your son, your only son, from me'" (vv. 10-12).

Sometimes, God will test our own hearts to see wherein we place our hope. Do we love God with all our heart? Do we find our hope, meaning, and significance in Him? As I mentioned at the beginning of the book, motherhood provides us opportunities to be changed and transformed. This is a good opportunity to explore the contents of your heart, to consider whether you might worship children and being a mother.

Gospel Truth: Identity in Christ

When children are an idol, it means we find our identity in motherhood. But that is not the source of our identity. As we looked at earlier, we are image bearers. We were created to image and reflect our Maker. We were made to worship, to glorify and enjoy God.

Though that image was broken by the Fall of Adam and Eve, God sent a second Adam, Jesus Christ, to live a perfect life on our behalf. Because He was perfect, He could also be a perfect sacrifice, taking our sins and bearing the punishment we deserved at the cross. Through faith in Christ and His perfect life, sacrificial death, and triumphant resurrection, we are united to Him and adopted into God's family. Christ's obedience is given to us. Because He obeyed in our place, because we are united to Him by faith, God looks at us and accepts us. We are now redeemed image bearers. We are being remade into the image of our Savior. That's our identity: we are 'in Christ.'

Being in Christ—being united to Him—is foundational to our faith. This amazing truth will take an eternity to plumb the depths of its significance. Paul often wrote about our unity with Christ in his epistles. Jesus spoke of that unity in John 15-17. Here are a few truths about what it means to be 'in Christ.'

It began in eternity past when God chose us in Christ. 'He chose us in him before the foundation of the world, that we should be holy and blameless before him' (Eph. 1:4).

In Christ, we have forgiveness. 'In him we have redemption through his blood, the forgiveness of our trespasses, according to the riches of his grace' (Eph. 1:7).

In Christ, we are sanctified. 'To those sanctified in Christ Jesus, called to be saints together with all those who in every place call upon the name of our Lord Jesus Christ, both their Lord and ours' (1 Cor. 1:2).

In Christ, we have been given the Spirit. 'In him you also, when you heard the word of truth, the gospel of your salvation, and believed in him, were sealed with the promised Holy Spirit, who is the guarantee of our inheritance until we acquire possession of it, to the praise of his glory' (Eph. 1:13-14).

In Christ, we are new creations. 'Therefore, if anyone is in Christ, he is a new creation. The old has passed away; behold, the new has come' (2 Cor. 5:17).

In Christ, we are loved. 'I in them and you in me, that they may become perfectly one, so that the world may know that you sent me and loved them even as you loved me' (John 17:23).

In Christ, we are united with other members of the Body. 'We, though many, are one body in Christ, and individually members one of another' (Rom. 12:5).

In Christ, we walk with Him. 'Therefore, as you received Christ Jesus the Lord, so walk in him, rooted and built up in him and established in the faith, just as you were taught, abounding in thanksgiving' (Col. 2:6-7).

In Christ, we have been raised. 'And raised us up with him and seated us with him in the heavenly places in Christ Jesus' (Eph. 2:6).

In Christ, we have peace. 'And the peace of God, which surpasses all understanding, will guard your hearts and your minds in Christ Jesus' (Phil. 4:7).

In Christ, we have all we need. 'And my God will supply every need of yours according to his riches in glory in Christ Jesus' (Phil. 4:19).

In Christ, we were made for good works. 'For we are his workmanship, created in Christ Jesus for good works, which God prepared beforehand, that we should walk in them' (Eph. 2:10).

Throughout the seasons of our lives much will change. The tasks and responsibilities we have today will be different than our tasks and responsibilities ten years from now. Indeed, we will spend a big part of our lives mothering our children. But it's not the only season of our lives. Whatever season we are in we have to remember that we are 'in Christ.' We are children of God. We are united with Christ and bear His image in the world. This identity shapes how we do the jobs, roles, and tasks God gives to us. It informs what it looks like for us to be wives, mothers, friends, daughters, church members, and co-workers. It defines how we love and serve others, including our children. This identity remains with us into eternity.

Rather than find our identity and meaning in motherhood, let's live out our identity as redeemed believers, as those who are 'in Christ.'

Questions for a Mother's Heart:

1. Go through the questions in chapter 4 to help you identify whether this is an idol of your heart. How do you use your time and money when it comes to your children? What are your fears regarding motherhood? What do you get angry about? What controls you? What are your 'if only's?

2. What desire does this idol meet for you?

3. Do you see how this idol might be considered an 'acceptable' sin in our culture and even in some Christian circles?

4. Read Ephesians 1. How many times does Paul use the phrase 'in Christ' or 'in Him?' What does it mean to you to be 'in Christ?'

A Prayer for a Mother's Heart:

Dear Father,

I come before you humbled as I realize the ways I have worshipped my children. A child is a good gift you give and rather than turn to you in gratitude for that gift, I have turned to it in worship.

Forgive me for seeking meaning and significance in my role as a mother. Forgive me for the sins I have committed in pursuing this idol. Forgive me for the sacrifices I have made to keep it.

I praise you for the truth that I am 'in Christ.' What amazing grace! I thank you that you look at me and see your Son. As I dwell on each truth about my union with Christ, I am filled with gratitude for all you have done. Help me to remember who I am because of what He has done.

In Jesus' precious name I pray,

Amen.

6

THE IDOL OF ACHIEVEMENT AND SUCCESS

The Mommy Wars. It's a term that's been tossed around for a few decades now. It re-emerges from time to time in the news, social media, and in the blogosphere and all the old conflicts and arguments re-emerge as well. What are the mommy wars? They are conflicts between women over aspects of parenting: breast feeding vs. bottle feeding, co-sleeping vs. crib sleeping, stay-at-home moms vs. working moms, etc. Moms take sides on these issues and stand their ground against other moms. There's finger-pointing, judgment, and criticism.

Scroll through social media and you will undoubtedly find statements made on one side or other of the mommy wars. A friend might post an article about why breast feeding is best for babies. You might notice another mom friend pin a number of posts related to co-sleeping. Or you might see a friend comment on someone's social media post, declaring their belief about some aspect of parenting. In all of it, you have some kind of emotional response. You might find yourself judging your friend for what they posted, or you might feel guilty because you do something different.

These mommy wars point to something many moms worship: achievement and success.

Idol of Achievement and Success

As moms, we want to get motherhood right. We research, study, plan, and prepare to learn the best way to raise our children. We want our children to be healthy, happy, and productive in life. We want them to have the best education. We want them to play the right sports. We want them to be the best dressed. As Christians, we want our children to obey us the first time, to love Jesus, serve others, and behave well—especially around other Christians.

If there's a book on parenting, we own it. We have subscriptions to all the parenting magazines. If we don't know what to do in a given situation, we look up the solution online. Whatever method we choose, we rest in that method. We put our hope in outcomes—in how our children behave, look, and in what they achieve.

We believe in the age-old belief that if you do things right, your life will be blessed. We take the parenting wisdom in the book of Proverbs as literal promises. We stake our lives on the belief that if we parent our child well—if we are a good mother—our child will turn out well. In Christianity, this means if we follow the right parenting model— take your pick which one that is—our children will be saved and grow up to honor God with their lives.

We always strive after what's next. When it's time for parent/teacher conferences at our child's school, we come prepared with a notepad and pen, ready to take notes on what we can do to help our child excel. In preschool we prepare our child for kindergarten, practicing their letters and numbers at every opportunity. When they are in elementary school, we think ahead to their middle school years, perhaps even getting them settled into the sport they will pursue and practice into their college years. In middle school, we prep them for high school. The high school years are focused on academic and athletic pursuits so they can get into the best college.

As parents, we want our child to be the best in the class, the top scorer on the team, and the one who knows all the catechism answers in Sunday school. So we push ourselves and our children to hit the mark. We don't rest until we've met our goals. We put our children in every activity possible, stressing them out and making them anxious. Not only that, but we exhaust ourselves trying to meet what our culture portrays as the image of a perfect mom.

When we worship success, our children become medals of sorts. We put them on display for all to see just how good a job we've done. If our children fail in some way, we take it personally. We get angry at them for embarrassing us. We feel let down as though the rule of life failed us. We think, 'How did that happen? I did everything right. My child is supposed to be ____, do ____, and achieve ____.' As Paul Tripp wrote, 'We begin to need them to be what they should be so that we can feel a sense of achievement and success. We begin to look at our children as our trophies rather than God's creatures. We secretly want to display them on the mantels of our lives as visible testimonies to a job well done. When they fail to live up to our expectations, we find ourselves not grieving for them and fighting for them, but angry at them, fighting against them, and, in fact, grieving for ourselves and our loss. We're angry because they've taken something valuable away from us, something we've come to treasure, something that has come to rule our hearts: a reputation for success.'[1]

Tim Keller defines the idol of success and achievement this way: 'personal success and achievement lead to a sense that we ourselves are god, that our security and value rest in our own wisdom, strength, and performance … One sign you have made success an idol is the false sense of security it brings … The false sense of security comes from deifying our achievement and expecting it to keep us safe from the troubles of life in a way that only God can.'[2] When we worship the idol of success and achievement, we trust in our parenting methods and our successes. We rest in our achievement rather than in the grace of God.

Comparing Ourselves and Our Children to Others

We all know her: the friend who has everything, the one who has it altogether. Her children are always perfectly dressed. Her house is beautiful and her children's playroom is just what you've always wanted. Her husband is quick

---

1. Paul Tripp Ministries. https://www.paultripp.com/articles/posts/the-idol-of-success (accessed April 25, 2017).

2. Keller, Timothy, *Counterfeit Gods: The Empty Promises of Money, Sex, and Power, and the Only Hope that Matters* (New York, NY: Dutton, 2009), p. 75.

to help out with the kids. She has her children involved in many activities. They always have the newest toys.

Every time you take your children to her house to play with her children, you always walk away thinking, 'Her son seems ahead of mine in development. Should I be doing something different? I love the way she dresses her daughter. I need to find out where she shops. I wish we had the play space she has. She signed her son up for soccer; I need to sign mine up too...'

Comparison. We all do it. We all compare ourselves, our children, our family, our experiences, and our possessions to what others have. When a friend's child starts crawling at six months, we wonder what's wrong with our child who seems content to simply roll from place to place. A friend might put their child in a particular school and we wonder if we should do the same. We compare our parenting techniques to theirs. We see the craft activities our friends share online and we feel like a failure because our idea of craft time with our children consists of a box of crayons and a stack of paper.

I've looked at friends who seem to have it all and wished I could wear their shoes, at least for a day. I've admired friends' home-school rooms and wanted the same for myself. I've taken note of my friend's son's development and measured my child's against it. I've scrolled through social media and wondered why my life isn't as exciting as that of my friends. Secretly, I've wished to find a chink in their armor, an imperfection of some kind, to let me know they aren't as perfect as they seem. Sometimes, I do see their weaknesses and find pleasure in knowing their life isn't so perfect after all.

Such comparison is rooted in the idol of success and achievement. We compare ourselves to others because we always seek to get things right. As Kyle Idleman noted, 'the god of achievement offers a method of measurement.'[3] We like to know where we stand. Have we gotten parenting right? We look to others to see how we are doing. We feel good about ourselves if we are doing better than others and pat ourselves on the back for a job well done. And if we don't measure up, we feel guilty and find ourselves working that much harder, chasing after parenting success.

Criticism of others

Another aspect to the idol of success and achievement is seen most notably in the mommy wars mentioned above. As moms, we are quick to critique and criticize other moms' choices in their mothering. We look down on those who don't do what we think is right. We get frustrated with people who don't work hard enough in their mothering. We have little patience for those who don't bother to do their research and understand all the issues.

We put people in boxes. Just one look at a mom and we know right away whether she is permissive or strict, uses television as a babysitter or not, or whether she nurses on demand or sticks to a schedule. We look at moms who parent differently than we do and decide they just aren't people we want to be associated with. If we learn that a friend believes differently than we do on a matter of parenting, we see her in a new light and it's not flattering. At the grocery store, when we see a toddler having a tantrum,

3. Idleman, Kyle, *Gods at War: Defeating the Idols that Battle for Your Heart* (Grand Rapids, MI: Zondervan, 2013), p. 174.

we watch to see how the mother responds. We put her in a box depending on what she does.

This criticism spreads far and wide. Our parents are critical of our parenting. We in turn are critical of how they parented us. We criticize the rich and famous for their parenting decisions splashed across the tabloids. We criticize people for what they post on social media. We criticize strangers in the street who let their children climb over everything, neighbors who don't know where their children are at any given time, and friends who let their children eat refined sugar. Sometimes this criticism is voiced aloud to the culprits, sometimes we voice it in whispers to other friends, and other times we keep it to ourselves (all the while feeling superior because we know the secret to successful parenting).

Such criticism separates us from others. Rather than being a help and support to one another in our parenting, moms become competitors. We treat each other like we are on different teams, as though there is some prize out there and only one of us can get it. Instead of encouraging and building one another up, we tear each other down with our gossip and belittling comments.

Biblical Success

Success in the Bible is different from that in the world. The world looks at success in terms of numbers—dollars and cents, followers, years of experience, market value, percentage on a test, etc. When it comes to parenting, the world views success as how our children turn out, whether they are healthy, happy, and a functioning member of society. Even better, parents are counted successful if their children get into a good college, get a good job, and make a good salary. And there are multiple theories on just how to do that.

In contrast, the Bible looks at success as fulfilling God's Kingdom purposes. As living to serve rather than be served. As obeying God even when no one else does. As living in the light when all around is darkness. As dying to self. Biblical success is found in meekness, humility, obedience, sacrifice, and death.

God doesn't look for those who already have it together; He uses the weak and makes them strong. Take Mary for example. She was a young teen about to get married. Poor in the eyes of the world, her husband-to-be was just a carpenter. Yet God chose her to be the mother of the Savior. Jesus wasn't born in a castle and raised as royalty; rather, He was born in a stable and lived a life of poverty. While He had many followers at times during His ministry, in the end, He had eleven disciples who scattered when He needed them most.

Paul described this upside down perspective in 1 Corinthians 1:

> For consider your calling, brothers: not many of you were wise according to worldly standards, not many were powerful, not many were of noble birth. But God chose what is foolish in the world to shame the wise; God chose what is weak in the world to shame the strong; God chose what is low and despised in the world, even things that are not, to bring to nothing things that are, so that no human being might boast in the presence of God. And because of him you are in Christ Jesus, who became to us wisdom from God, righteousness and

sanctification and redemption, so that, as it is written,
'Let the one who boasts, boast in the Lord' (vv. 26-31).

We need to remember that success and achievement as
mothers looks different than what we read in the parenting magazines. It's different than what the moms in our
'mommy and me' classes are doing or what we perceive
is happening in the lives of others through social media.
Biblical success involves seeking God first and living for
His glory in all that we do. It is relying upon His grace to
live out our calling as mothers, not trusting in our own
strength, abilities, knowledge, or hard work. Ultimately,
our success is found in Christ. It is in Him that we boast.

Gospel Truth: Worthy in Christ

When we worship success and achievement, we seek to
find our worth in what we accomplish. Our successes have
the final say on our value. It's up to us and our efforts to
create that worth. The success idol is never satisfied, so we
have to keep striving, working, and reaching. If we stop,
fail, or our children don't turn out the way we expected,
our perceived worth shatters.

But the gospel tells us something different. God doesn't
love us because of anything we've done. Whether we are
the best mom in the cul-de-sac or our child's GPA places
him or her at the top of the class has no influence on what
God thinks of us. The truth is, there is nothing we can do
to make ourselves worthy to a holy and righteous God.
Because of sin, we were separated from God. We were
dead in our trespasses and sins. On our own, all we want,
desire, and seek after is sin.

But for the grace of God.

Ephesians tells us that God chose us before the foundation of the world (Eph. 1:4). He created us in His image. 'I praise you, for I am fearfully and wonderfully made. Wonderful are your works; my soul knows it very well' (Ps. 139:14).While we were still sinners, Christ died for us (Rom 5:8). The Spirit awakened us from death and gave us new life. We were given the gift of faith and saved from the penalty of our sins. 'For the wages of sin is death, but the free gift of God is eternal life in Christ Jesus our Lord' (Rom. 6:23). The Holy Spirit lives in us, comforting, guiding, and changing us. Christ our Lord intercedes to the Father for us, covering us with His righteousness. We are promised eternal life in the presence of God. All of this comes to us by the grace of God; we do nothing to earn or achieve it.

Moms, we have significant value and worth. But it's not based on what we achieve. It's not about our success as a mother. It's not about how well our children turn out. Our worth is grounded in who Christ is for us, and what He accomplished on our behalf.

Do you worship achievement and success? Do you find your worth in your parenting skills and achievements? Do you find your value in your child's performance? Take time to pray about this idol and ask the Spirit to help you identify whether this is an idol for you. Remember, you are worthy in Christ. You can't do anything to make Him love you any more than He does right now. If you fail in your parenting, He won't love you any less. Rest in this today.

Questions for a Mother's Heart:

1. Have you ever compared your life to other moms you know? What happens in your heart when your life seems less in comparison?

2. Do you critique other moms? Why do you suppose their decisions matter so much to you?

3. Take time to think and pray through your thoughts regarding parenting success. How do you define success as a parent? What does it look like? What makes you feel successful as a parent? Do you believe you have to be successful in parenting? Do you believe that how well you do as a parent has a direct correlation to how well your child does in life? How do God's redemptive purposes in our lives and in the lives of our children work into that belief?

4. Consider your emotional responses. Do you find yourself getting angry with other moms, especially when they make a different parenting decision than you? How do you respond when your child fails at something? How about when you fail in some area of parenting?

5. Read Philippians 2:1-11. How are we to be like Christ? What does this look like in our attitudes and behavior toward other moms?

A Prayer for a Mother's Heart:

Dear Father,

Just today, I found myself relishing and glorying in my child's success. I see now how I have compared myself and my children to others. I even see how I have looked down on other moms for not mothering the same way that I do.

Forgive me for this. Forgive me for finding my worth in success. Forgive me for seeking the accolades and affirmation of others.

I thank you that I am worthy in Christ. I thank you that Jesus did not count equality with You a 'thing to be grasped, but emptied himself, by taking the form of a servant, being born in the likeness of men. And being found in human form, he humbled himself by becoming obedient to the point of death, even death on a cross' (Phil. 2:6-8). I thank you that He did not seek out success as the world sees it but laid down His life for me, so that His success would be mine.

Help me to fight this idol of success through the work and grace of the Spirit.

In Jesus' name,

Amen.

7

THE IDOL OF COMFORT

Does this scenario sound familiar?

The kids have been sick for days. At first, it was one child who picked up something in the church nursery. You stayed up all night comforting him and giving medicine every few hours. Before long, another child came down sick. And then another.

You are exhausted. You're tired of being stuck at home. The kids are irritable and clingy. Your husband is out of town for work and the minutes seem to stretch out long until his return.

You look forward to the end of the day, counting down the hours until bedtime. What you want most is a bowl of your favorite frozen treat and to zone out in front of the television. In fact, after the crazy last couple of days you've had, you deserve time to yourself to do what you want to do. You need some 'me time.' Right?

Perhaps it's not a bowl of ice cream or an entire season of your favorite drama you look forward to. Maybe you desire something else. Maybe it's a grande latte. Or it might be an afternoon shopping at the mall. It might be a day at the spa. It might be escaping into the pages of a book. It might be scrolling through Facebook or Instagram. Whatever it is, you seek that thing to give you pleasure and comfort.

As a mom, I have found myself in that place of weariness and exhaustion. I have found myself tired of the mundane duties of motherhood, of having to repeat the same instruction and the same lesson over and over again—only to rinse and repeat again the next day. I have felt lonely and isolated and taken for granted. In those moments, I've found myself tempted to turn to some thing to give me comfort. Sometimes it's been a sweet treat. Other times, it's been a shopping trip. I've found myself reaching for a soda or coffee in the afternoon and thinking, 'I deserve this after the day I've had.'

My children are not little anymore and they don't exhaust me to the level they did when they were younger, but even now I find myself at the end of the day wanting to be by myself so I can zone out in front of the television. It's part of my evening routine that I look forward to. It's sacred. And it's mine.

The Idol of Comfort

Comfort and pleasure are the gods of this age and our world. Commercials and advertisements seek to woo us into purchasing whatever pleasure they are selling. Everyone looks happy and carefree enjoying their product. Grocery stores and restaurants use words like 'comfort food' 'juicy' 'rich and decadent' 'guilty pleasure' to entice us. We can stream entire seasons of a television show and watch it all in one sitting, if we so desire. The opportunities for entertainment are endless. There are more ways to spend money on ourselves than ever before. And we don't have to wait long; everything can be downloaded in an instant or shipped to our door in less than twenty-four hours.

In our culture, pleasure is considered a right. Whatever it is we want, society says we should pursue it with full gusto. Watch any television show and inevitably, someone will talk to a friend about a decision they have to make. The response is always, 'What will make you happy?' The pursuit of happiness is a priority over commitments, responsibilities, and the needs of others. No matter the consequences, going after our pleasures is seen as the most important thing we can do for ourselves. We see this in how people live out their sexuality, use their money, spend their time, and what they ingest into their bodies. For some, the pursuit of pleasure and comfort grows into an addiction, one which takes over and rules their lives.

Such pleasures serve as an anesthetic to the soul.[1] They numb us to the harsh realities of life. They are temporary rewards to the trials and troubles of our days. For a time, they make us forget. They distract us and help us escape from real life. For some, they give meaning to the dry, mundane boredom of life. For others, comfort and pleasure mask the painful circumstances they face. And for still others, pleasure serves as a fitting co-host to a pity party.

Motherhood is filled with reasons why we would want to escape, numb ourselves, or find pleasure in something. Perhaps we thought we'd find our happiness in motherhood, but our expectations proved wrong. We might have a child with unique problems or needs—needs we feel inadequate to handle. We might feel alone without help and support. Or maybe we find motherhood boring, hard, or unrewarding. Our life as a mother might be stressful and exhausting. Whatever the reason, this idol tells us we deserve pleasure. We deserve distraction and escape. We need it in order to find happiness.

The problem with the idol of comfort is that it is never filled and never satisfied. It is like a bucket with a hole in the bottom. We keep filling it and it immediately empties back out. That gallon of ice cream only lasts so long and then it's gone. We can escape to Facebook until the baby wakes and then reality crashes upon us. The show we are watching eventually comes to an end. And we are still the same person with the same problems. The idol of comfort only provides a temporary stay. It can never fill

---

1. Allender, Dan B. and Longman, Tremper III, *Breaking the Idols of Your Heart: How to Navigate the Temptations of Life* (Downers Grove, IL: Intervarsity Press, 2007), p. 100.

the void. That's why we find ourselves having to have more and more of whatever that pleasure is. It's an idol whose hunger is never satiated. As Allender and Longman write, 'When life is hard, pleasure can be more than a diversion. It can easily become a need. We easily move from a properly moderate enjoyment of sensuous experience to a consuming desire for it.'[2]

Another problem with the idol of comfort is that we start to think we have a right to pleasure and comfort. We deserve it. So we structure our days around it. We demand it. When something or someone keeps us from our pleasures, we respond in anger. We start to resent those who interfere. That child who refuses to nap becomes an obstacle to our sacred Netflix time. We finally sit down at the end of the day and hear, 'Mom!' We sigh in irritation because in our mind we had clocked out for the day.

The idol of comfort also keeps us from our responsibilities. We find ourselves watching one episode after another instead of playing with our toddler. We scroll through social media countless times during the day, looking at the lives of our friends rather than living our own life. The more we pursue our comforts and pleasures, the more they pursue us. We let others down and fail to keep up with our daily tasks because our pleasures have become our taskmaster.

Pleasure Points us to God

Don't get me wrong. Pleasure isn't a bad thing. All the good things we enjoy in life are gifts from God. The food

---

2. Ibid., p. 102.

we eat, the entertainment we enjoy, the laughter and fun we have with others—these are all good things. God gives us good things because He loves us. He didn't have to create us with senses. He didn't have to make us with the ability to smell roasted coffee beans or taste the salty-sweet goodness of salted caramel ice cream. But He did. They are blessings for us to enjoy. 'You cause the grass to grow for the livestock and plants for man to cultivate, that he may bring forth food from the earth and wine to gladden the heart of man, oil to make his face shine and bread to strengthen man's heart' (Ps. 104:14-15). 'If you then, who are evil, know how to give good gifts to your children, how much more will your Father who is in heaven give good things to those who ask him!' (Matt. 7:11).

Indeed, God promises us rewards and pleasures both in this life and the life to come. He promises to meet our needs in the here and now. He promises to be with us and never forsake us. He gave us the gift of His Spirit who comforts, encourages, instructs, convicts, and teaches us. He also made us heirs with Christ of His Kingdom. Like the Levites, our inheritance is not a piece of land, rather it is God Himself. Christ purchased for us eternal life in the presence of God. 'In my Father's house are many rooms. If it were not so, would I have told you that I go to prepare a place for you? And if I go and prepare a place for you, I will come again and will take you to myself, that where I am you may be also' (John 14: 2-3).

The pleasures God promises us in Christ are richer and more satisfying than anything we enjoy now. As C.S. Lewis wrote, 'if we consider the unblushing promises of reward and the staggering nature of the rewards promised in the

Gospels, it would seem that Our Lord finds our desires not too strong, but too weak. We are half-hearted creatures, fooling about with drink and sex and ambition when infinite joy is offered us, like an ignorant child who wants to go on making mud pies in a slum because he cannot imagine what is meant by the offer of a holiday at the sea. We are far too easily pleased.'[3]

Ultimately, all God's gifts are given to point us to Himself. The things we enjoy in this life are meant to remind us of the goodness of God. They are to give us a taste of the greater joy that awaits us in eternity. Such pleasure 'enriches the heart and body while also, paradoxically, causing the heart to hunger, to ache for what no earthly pleasure can provide: a direct, consuming encounter with God.'[4]

The things we taste, the things we feel, the things we experience, all the things we enjoy are meant to ultimately help us enjoy and know more of God. Physical pleasures help us appreciate and understand spiritual pleasures. 'Apart from our experience of empty stomachs and parched throats, of full bellies, quenched thirsts, and the incredible variety of taste, our spiritual lives would be impoverished, and we would have no real vocabulary for spiritual desire, no mental and emotional framework for engaging with God.'[5] Because of this, John 6:51 makes sense, 'I am the living bread that came down from heaven. If anyone eats

---

3. Lewis, C.S., *The Weight of Glory* (New York, NY: HarperCollins, 1949), p. 26.

4. Allender and Longman, pp. 102-103.

5. Rigney, Joe, *The Things of Earth: Treasuring God by Enjoying His Gifts* (Wheaton, IL: Crossway, 2015), p. 81.

of this bread, he will live forever. And the bread that I will give for the life of the world is my flesh.' Since we know the sweet taste of honey, we can relate to David's words, 'How sweet are your words to my taste, sweeter than honey to my mouth!' (Ps. 119:103).

The problem is that when comfort is an idol, we love the gifts of God rather than the giver—God Himself. We turn to the gift as though it is our savior. Rather than taking God's gifts with gratitude and thanking Him, we treat such gifts as a right and demand them. We are like Veruca Salt in Roald Dahl's story, *Charlie and the Chocolate Factory*. She was the epitome of a spoiled and overindulged child who told her father what she wanted, and expected to receive it right then and there. In the movie adaptation of the book, she sang, 'I want a ball. I want a party. Pink macaroons and a million balloons and performing baboons. Give it to me now. I want the world, I want the whole world. I want to lock it all up in my pocket. It's my bar of chocolate. Give it to me now!'[6]

As moms, we can enjoy time to ourselves. Having time of quiet and rest and relaxation is important. Our bodies and minds need rest. During that time, we can certainly enjoy a cup of coffee or some other pleasure. For some, it might mean going for a walk or run. For others, it might mean working on a hobby or pursuing a creative outlet. It could mean baking a loaf of bread or painting on a canvas. It might mean reading a book or talking to a friend. Yet, whatever we do to enjoy time to ourselves can't be

---

6. *Willie Wonka and the Chocolate Factory.* Dir. Mel Stuart. Paramount, 1971. Film.

where we place our hope. It can't be what we turn to as a distraction to our hopelessness. It can't be what fills our emptiness.

Moms, we do need breaks. We need help and hope in the hard days of motherhood. So when we take time to rest, let's also take time to turn to God and seek after Him. We can seek Him in prayer, telling Him the struggles of our day, our fears about our children, and how alone we feel. We can tell Him that we feel inadequate to the task and helpless in our mothering. We can cry out to Him, asking for wisdom, grace, and strength.

Our God hears us because we are united to Christ. We can trust Him to be for us what we cannot be for ourselves. Let's take time to turn to His word and be reminded afresh of God's great love for us in Christ. Rather than turning to a substitute god to give us temporary happiness, let us turn to the only One who gives us true joy, '... in your presence there is fullness of joy; at your right hand are pleasures forevermore' (Ps. 16:11).

Gospel Truth: Joy in Christ

When we worship comfort and pleasure, we are seeking joy and happiness in something that can never give us joy. Deep, lasting joy is found only in Christ:

> Blessed be the God and Father of our Lord Jesus Christ! According to his great mercy, he has caused us to be born again to a living hope through the resurrection of Jesus Christ from the dead, to an inheritance that is imperishable, undefiled, and unfading, kept in heaven for you, who by God's power are being guarded through faith for a salvation ready to be revealed in the last

time. In this you rejoice, though now for a little while, if necessary, you have been grieved by various trials, so that the tested genuineness of your faith—more precious than gold that perishes though it is tested by fire—may be found to result in praise and glory and honor at the revelation of Jesus Christ. Though you have not seen him, you love him. Though you do not now see him, you believe in him and rejoice with joy that is inexpressible and filled with glory, obtaining the outcome of your faith, the salvation of your souls (1 Pet. 1:3-9).

Our joy doesn't come from within ourselves. We can't create it. It's not found in something made. It's found in Christ. Our joy is found in knowing Him and being known by Him. In fact, eternal life is knowing God: 'And this is eternal life, that they know you, the only true God, and Jesus Christ whom you have sent' (John 17:3).

This joy is not dependent upon circumstances, but is rooted in what Christ has done for us. It is joy that takes the arm of other emotions, like fear and sorrow, and accompanies them into the trials and hardships of life. It is joy that is comfortable with weeping yet whose tears do not cloud its vision because it knows that glory rises on the other side of trials. Unattached to the world, this joy looks to another, to eternity where we will live forever in the presence of our Savior. As Peter wrote, this joy is inexpressible—there are no words in the human tongue to describe it— as we consider the day when our salvation is complete in glory.

Moms, let us seek to know more of this joy. Let's take time to read and reflect on the rich promises for us found in God's Word. Let's set our minds on things above and dwell on our hope and eternal inheritance in eternity. Let's remember what Christ is doing in us through His Spirit and how He is preparing us for the day when we meet Him face to face. Let's rejoice in our salvation and God's great love for us in Christ. And may our hearts be happy as we consider our inheritance found in God Himself.

Questions for a Mother's Heart:

1. Do you find yourself using your time toward the pursuit of comfort and pleasure? Do you ever find yourself feeling sorry for yourself? Do you find yourself stressed by the challenges of motherhood? Do you turn to the idol of comfort during that time?

2. What is happiness? Is it something found in the gifts God gives us? How have you turned to the gift rather than the Giver for hope and happiness?

3. How have you failed to give thanks to God for the gifts He has given you? Take time to pray and respond to Him with thanksgiving.

4. In Scripture, the word 'blessed' (in Greek, *makarios*) is the same as 'happy.'[7] Read Matthew 5:1-12 and substitute the word 'happy' for 'blessed.' How is that different from what the world says about happiness?

---

7. Study Light. https://www.studylight.org/language-studies/greek-thoughts /index.cgi?a=10#F1 (accessed June 10, 2017).

A Prayer for a Mother's Heart:

Dear Father,

I come before you today worn out from a long day with the kids. It was a hard day. I find myself staring at the freezer, wanting comfort in a gallon of ice cream. I just want to hide away in my room in front of the television and forget about the day.

Father, I am so drawn to comfort. It is an idol that reels me in every day. Especially on really hard days. Forgive me for seeking hope and joy in things you've made rather than in you. I thank you for the pleasures you have created. Help me to enjoy you through them.

Help me to turn to you when I am weary or stressed. Help me to seek you as my refuge, not a mindless television show or a sale at the store.

In Jesus' name,

Amen.

8

THE IDOL OF CONTROL

In the beginning of this book, I described motherhood for me as a whirlwind. One of those whirlwinds was my children's health. My oldest son started having health problems around eighteen months old. He had a horrible sounding cough that just wouldn't go away. We soon learned he had asthma. Then he got one sinus infection after another which further aggravated his asthma. We spent a couple of years in and out of specialists. Yet my son never got better.

His wheezing cough would wake us up in the middle of the night. We'd give him breathing treatments and make an appointment to see the doctor the next morning. We'd inevitably learn that he had another infection. The problem was, it's not healthy for our bodies to be on antibiotics for an extended period of time. After a year and a half of the constant cycle of illness and medication, the doctors finally decided that my son needed sinus surgery. At the time, it was a risky procedure for a four-year-old. We had to travel to a specialist who was willing to do it. How fearful I was waiting at the hospital while my son was in surgery! The surgery worked and he has been healthy ever since.

During that season of chronic illness, I found myself always on edge. I felt helpless. I worried, stressed, and fretted about my son's health. When he was around other kids who were coughing or had runny noses, I nearly panicked, thinking, 'Great. Now he'll get sick and have another asthma attack.'

Motherhood during that time was a constant state of helplessness, fear, and worry. Life felt like it was out of my control. No matter what I did, I couldn't help my child. It only made matters worse when my youngest son had the same health problems—only his asthma made an appearance when he was six weeks old. With two children experiencing the same problems, I was always worried about their health. I wondered if there was something I was missing. I researched online, read forums, and explored all the possibilities. I even hired a mold inspector to come and thoroughly inspect every inch of our house to see if mold was causing their chronic infections.

I think most of us as moms have felt worry at some point over our child's health. I think we all can relate to feeling helpless the first time our little one wakens us in the night with a cough or fever. Who hasn't called the doctor right away for the littlest thing?

But health isn't the only area of motherhood where we might feel such helplessness. We might feel helpless because we have a child with some kind of disability. Perhaps they have a physical limitation. Or maybe they have trouble with some aspect of learning. Maybe we feel helpless because the developmental stage our child is in is particularly challenging and hard. Our helplessness might come because our finances are tight and we can't provide for our children in the way we need. We might be in a schooling situation that isn't ideal and we can't find a way to change it. Whatever our circumstances or situations, we all know the feeling of helplessness as a mother.

For some of us, the feeling of helplessness, and our response to that helplessness, reveals an idol in our hearts: the idol of control.

The Idol of Control

The idol of control involves a desire for things to go according to *our* will and plan. We have expectations and seek to make certain they come to pass. We do whatever it takes to manage and rule over our lives. We dislike chaos and disorder. Not knowing what will happen next and feelings of uncertainty put us on edge.

When we worship the idol of control, we often find ourselves filled with worry. We lie awake at night trying to anticipate what will happen next and develop strategies for how to handle it. We live by our to-do lists, personal rules, routines, plans, and strategies. Google is our constant companion.

The idol of control tells us that we ought to be able to control and order our lives. This is our belief and we live by it. As a result, we are always seeking a new method or strategy. Scroll through Pinterest or read any of the mommy blogs online and you'll see that this desire is common among mothers. You'll find titles for articles such as: '5 Ways to get Your Child to Eat More Vegetables,' '3 Ways to Handle Tantrums,' '10 Things Your Child Needs From You,' and '12 Ways to Raise a Happy Child.' We are drawn to solutions such as these. We put our hope in them, following them to the letter. We trust these methods to make our lives—and our children—manageable.

Allender and Longman point out, 'We all want control over the chaos of our lives. We don't like unwelcome surprises, and we plan and work hard to keep them at bay. We think ahead about the consequences of our actions, and we are not pleased when someone—a child, a friend, a stranger—disrupts whatever order we've established in our lives.'[1]

For moms who worship the idol of control, it can look different from one mother to the next. For some, we might strive to control and manage the health of our children, as in my example above. We might be vigilant about our children's diet, about making sure they wash their hands, and in keeping them away from other sick children. For others, we might seek control through the way we order and structure our days. We live by our routines and won't permit any interruptions to our carefully designed schedule. Other moms might worship control through their rules, discipline, and instruction of their children.

---

1. Allender, Dan B. and Longman, Tremper III, *Breaking the Idols of Your Heart: How to Navigate the Temptations of Life* (Downers Grove, IL: Intervarsity Press, 2007), p. 27.

It's easy to control things when our children are little. We determine when and what they will eat, what they will wear, what they will do, and who they will spend time with. As they get older, they start making more choices of their own. They choose their own clothes to wear, their own friends, and their own activities. Eventually, all their choices are made on their own. Though this process is normal, it is hard for moms to let go of control over their children. We fear they will make poor choices and worse, we fear the consequences to those choices.

Rules, structure, goals, and plans are all good things. The Bible has rules for us: The Ten Commandments. It even encourages making plans and thinking through things before we act. 'The plans of the diligent lead surely to abundance, but everyone who is hasty comes only to poverty' (Prov. 21:5). The Bible frowns on lack of self-control and self-discipline. 'A man without self-control is like a city broken into and left without walls' (Prov. 25:28). Self-control is something we are to desire and in fact is a fruit of the Spirit at work in us (Gal. 5:22-23).

The problem with the idol of control is that our rules, plans, and desire to control things end up ruling us. We become slaves to the idol of control. We see this most vividly when our lives are out of control. When our plans fail, when something or someone cuts into our routine, or when we are surprised by the storms of life, how we react reveals the grip the idol of control has on our hearts. We respond in worry and fear, as I did with my children's chronic illness. We respond in anger toward those who interrupt our plans. We try to exert power and influence over others in an effort to control them. Our desire for control even interferes with our relationships, causing us to value our routines over the needs of others.

Taking Control vs. Dependency

An example of taking control is found in the story of Abram and Sarai. In Genesis 12, God called Abram to Himself. He promised to make him into a great nation. Abram packed up his family and possessions and followed God where He led him. Several times God reaffirmed this promise. In Genesis 15, God made a covenant with Abram, saying, 'Look toward heaven, and number the stars, if you are able to number them.' Then he said to him, 'So shall your offspring be' (Gen. 15:5).

The problem was, Abram and his wife Sarai were old. Sarai was past child-bearing age. God had promised them an heir and made a covenant with them that their descendants would be as many as the stars in the sky. But nothing had happened; she was still barren.

So Sarai took control of the situation. She gave her servant Hagar to Abram and said, 'Behold now, the LORD has prevented me from bearing children. Go in to my servant; it may be that I shall obtain children by her' (Gen. 16:2). Sarai didn't trust that God would keep His promise so she found a way to make it happen herself.

How often do we do the same? How often do we give up on waiting on the Lord and instead take control of the situations in our life?

This desire to rule over our lives is nothing new. Such desire for control began in the Garden with our first parents. When Satan told Eve that if she ate from the tree, her eyes would be opened and she would be like God, the

Bible tells us, 'the woman saw that the tree was good for food, and that it was a delight to the eyes, and that the tree was to be desired to make one wise' (Gen. 3:6). Tim Keller wrote, 'The original temptation in the Garden of Eden was to resent the limits God had put on us ... and to seek to be "as God" by taking power over our own destiny. We gave in to this temptation and now it is part of our nature. Rather than accept our finitude and dependence on God, we desperately seek ways to assure ourselves that we still have power over our own lives.'[2]

The truth is, we do not have control over our lives. We are not goddesses. We are dependent creatures. We are children reliant and dependent upon our heavenly Father. 'The God who made the world and everything in it, being Lord of heaven and earth, does not live in temples made by man, nor is he served by human hands, as though he needed anything, since he himself gives to all mankind life and breath and everything' (Acts 17:24-25). Everything comes to us by the grace of God. Everything. The fact that we wake up each morning is a gift of grace. We don't keep our bodies alive and functioning each day. We don't determine the number of our days. We don't even know the number of hairs on our head. But God does. Our idolatry of control is a resistance to our dependency upon God and His grace in our lives. We think we know better. We have a better plan for our lives. We don't like the story God has written and want to take over as author. But that's impossible because we are not God.

---

2. Keller, Timothy, *Counterfeit Gods: The Empty Promises of Money, Sex, and Power, and the Only Hope that Matters* (New York, NY: Dutton, 2009), p. 101.

God is the One who rules and reigns over all things. He is sovereign and in control. Our plans are subject to His rule and will. 'The heart of man plans his way, but the LORD establishes his steps' (Prov. 16:9). 'The king's heart is a stream of water in the hand of the LORD; he turns it wherever he will' (Prov. 21:1).

God's purposes will stand; nothing and no one can interfere with God's will. 'For I am God, and there is no other; I am God, and there is none like me, declaring the end from the beginning and from ancient times things not yet done, saying, "My counsel shall stand, and I will accomplish all my purpose," calling a bird of prey from the east, the man of my counsel from a far country. I have spoken, and I will bring it to pass; I have purposed, and I will do it' (Isa. 46:9-11).

There is no such thing as chance or coincidence. Even things that seem random to us are in fact under God's control. 'The lot is cast into the lap, but its every decision is from the LORD' (Prov. 16:33). God rules over all of creation, over the hearts of man, over time and history itself—nothing is outside of His sovereign control.

The Heidelberg Catechism puts it beautifully: 'God's providence is his almighty and ever present power, whereby, as with his hand, he still upholds heaven and earth and all creatures, and so governs them that leaf and blade, rain and drought, fruitful and barren years, food and drink, health and sickness, riches and poverty, indeed, all things, come to us not by chance but by his fatherly hand.'[3]

---

3. Heidelberg Catechism http://www.heidelberg-catechism.com/en/lords-days/10.html (accessed June 10, 2017).

Moms, we must learn to rest in God's sovereignty. It must become a comfort to us. Our God is holy, perfect, righteous, and good. He always does what is just and true. He always acts with wisdom; He always does what is right. We can trust His sovereign control over our lives and that of our children. We need to yield in dependence and humble reliance upon His sovereignty. As the Heidelberg Catechism teaches, because God is in control, 'We can be patient in adversity, thankful in prosperity, and with a view to the future we can have a firm confidence in our faithful God and Father that no creature shall separate us from his love; for all creatures are so completely in his hand that without his will they cannot so much as move.'[4]

Gospel Truth: Security in Christ

When we worship the idol of control, we seek security in something other than God. We place our hope for safety in ourselves or some method or rule. Scripture tells us God alone is our safety and security. 'The LORD is my rock and my fortress and my deliverer, my God, my rock, in whom I take refuge, my shield, and the horn of my salvation, my stronghold' (Ps. 18:2). 'In peace I will both lie down and sleep; for you alone, O LORD, make me dwell in safety' (Ps. 4:8). 'Blessed is he whose help is the God of Jacob, whose hope is in the LORD his God' (Ps. 146:5).

When the psalmist referred to God as his salvation, he was ultimately writing about Christ. He is the promised Rescuer the Old Testament writers pointed forward to. He is the one who saves and rescues us from sin and evil. He

---

4. Ibid.

is our refuge, our fortress, our deliverer. Because of Christ, we can come to the throne of grace in confidence and receive help from our Father in heaven.

We can turn to our Savior with all our fears. When we worry for our children, when we fear the unknown, when we feel helpless as a mother, we can turn to Christ. We can cry out to Him. We can tell Him our fears and our worries. We can tell Him that we just don't know what to do. We can ask for help and wisdom in our troubles as a mother. We can pray for whatever is on our heart and know that God hears us. In fact, He knows what we need before we even ask it. We need to trust in Him to be our help and remember that there is no method, rule, or plan that can give us lasting hope. Everything else will fail us; Christ never will.

In addition to turning to God in prayer, we also need to remember who God is and what He has done for us in Christ. 'Let us hold fast the confession of our hope without wavering, for he who promised is faithful' (Heb. 10:23). Our God is faithful. He promised to send a Savior and He did. We need to steep our hearts in the Word, reading and rereading what God did for us by sending His Son to redeem us from sin. If God rescued us from our worst fear—eternal separation from Him—how can He not also deliver us from our current fears? How can we think that He would leave us on our own in our daily problems? God went to great lengths to rescue us from death, going so far as to send His Son to die for us. He has proven Himself faithful. How can we not trust Him to be faithful in our lives right now? The truths of the gospel, of who Christ is and what He has done, are our confession of hope. They are our security; they anchor us in the storms of life and in the chaos of motherhood.

Do you worship the idol of control? Pray for wisdom to identify this idol in your heart. Consider the desires of your heart, your strongest emotions, and what you believe about the chaos of life. Turn to your Father in heaven and give Him your fears. Trust in your faithful God who never ceases to do what is good for you.

Questions for a Mother's Heart:

1. What chaos in your life do you find yourself trying to manage?

2. What are your fears? In what ways do you try to control the things you fear?

3. Read and study about God's goodness (Ps. 25:8-10, Ps. 145:17, Titus 3:3-7). Because God is good, all of His plans for us and for our children are good. Do you believe this?

A Prayer for a Mother's Heart:

My Father in heaven,

I come before you today filled with worries and fears. Life is chaotic and out of control. I find myself trying so hard to manage it all. I can't rest for all the worry.

Forgive me for worshipping the idol of control. Forgive me for thinking I can be master over my life. Forgive me for not trusting you as ruler over all things.

You are a good Father. You only do what is good for me and my children. Help me to rest in and trust in this truth. Help me to face my fears with this truth.

Please hear my cries this day about the chaos of our lives. I pray you would rule and reign over this situation. May your will be done on earth as it is in heaven.

Because of Jesus I pray,

Amen.

9

THE IDOL OF APPROVAL

Do you remember your first day of middle school or high school? Do you remember those mixed feelings of anticipation and fear? Both the excitement and the dread? For many, the adolescent years are shaping years. The experiences we have during that time help mold us into who we are today. They can also be tortuous years. Adolescents find themselves placed into groups based on social status. They are either 'in' or 'out.' They are either popular or not. Many strive to seek approval of other teens in the way they dress, talk, who they spend time with, their interests, and more. For some, no matter how hard they try to be accepted, they only fail. These teens often end up teased, mocked, and rejected—cast aside as though worthless.

There's a movie from the 1980's titled, 'The Breakfast Club.' In this movie, a group of teens had to spend a Saturday in detention as a form of punishment for various infractions at their school. Their assignment during the detention was to write a paper about who they think they are. Each of the teens was different: one was pretty and popular, another was an athlete, another a nerd, another a delinquent, and another was so lost she didn't even earn detention—she was there because she had nowhere else to be. In many ways, each of the teens longed for approval and acceptance and each one sought it out in different ways.

One of the students, Claire, was popular. Her popularity gave her life meaning. It was a popularity she worked hard to maintain. There were certain expectations she had to fulfill to remain in the popular crowd. As the movie went on, the characters bonded together despite their different statuses. And though she made friends with the others, in the end, Claire informed them she wouldn't acknowledge them if they crossed paths in the hall at school. Approval from her peers meant too much to her.

Though our adolescent years have long past, and though we might not break off into groups depending on our social status or standing among our peers, many of us still seek approval from others. We still desire acceptance and belonging.

The Idol of Approval

Here is a scenario with which we are all familiar: You are at church on a Sunday morning. The service is over and everyone is gathered for fellowship. Adults are drinking coffee; the children are drinking juice and munching on cookies. Your child walks up to the table where the drinks and snacks are laid out and reaches for a cookie. You step in and tell her she can't have a cookie because it will soon be lunch time. (You know from previous experience that if she snacks, she'll never eat her lunch.) As soon as you say the word, 'No,' she drops to the floor in a tantrum. Everyone in the church turns and looks at you. The other young moms in your Bible study watch to see what you will do. You are certain the older ladies gathered together are whispering about you. The sound of your child's screams echo off the walls. Your face reddens as you lean down to speak to your child. You can only imagine what everyone is thinking—and it's nothing good. (Okay, so maybe it's not a made-up story. Names and identities have been changed to protect the innocent.)

The idol of approval involves a longing to be accepted by others. It comes from the belief that we must be loved or accepted in order for life to have meaning. When people affirm us, give us attention, and show their approval, we feel good. We feel right. We belong and are important. But when people do not show their approval, we are devastated. We feel empty and meaningless. Worthless.

When we worship the idol of approval, we care most what others think of us. We want them to think highly of us, to like us. For moms, worshipping the idol of approval means we care deeply what other people think of how we are doing as a mom. Our meaning is dependent upon what they think. We want others to say we are doing a good job. We desire comments approving of our parenting techniques and our children's behavior. We want compliments on the new dress we bought our daughter or the cute bow tie we purchased for our infant son. We love when people say how integral and important our child is to the soccer team. We love hearing about how bright, polite, well-behaved, or beautiful our child is.

As a mom, I've found myself worshipping the idol of approval. When my kids were preschoolers, I loved when teachers commented to me about how bright and smart my children were. When other young moms asked me for parenting advice, I felt significant and important. But when people critiqued parenting decisions I made, gave me unsolicited advice, or failed to affirm me as a parent, I found myself crushed and disappointed. I did whatever I could to get their approval.

What an approval worshipper fears most is losing the approval of others. We fear their judgment, critique, dislike, and rejection. Because our meaning and worth is wrapped up in what others think, it's a constant roller coaster. Our value as a person rises and plummets based on the thoughts of others. The Bible calls this the fear of man. 'The fear of man lays a snare, but whoever trusts in the LORD is safe' (Prov. 29:25). Ed Welch wrote, 'Peer pressure, codependency, shame, low self-esteem—these are some of the words used to identify how you can be controlled by the perceived opinions of others. You could even use the phrase "fear of other people" to describe the experience. When you fear something you are controlled by it. If you fear people, you are controlled by people. It's as if the opinions of other people are a threat to you. You are always looking for ways to ward off their life-threatening rejection.'[1]

Peter feared those gathered in the high priest's courtyard the night Jesus was arrested. He feared what they thought of him and his association with Christ. Each time someone asked him if he knew Jesus, he denied it. 'But he began to invoke a curse on himself and to swear, "I do not know this man of whom you speak"' (Mark 14:71).

John commented on why people fear man, 'Nevertheless, many even of the authorities believed in him, but for fear of the Pharisees they did not confess it, so that they would not be put out of the synagogue; *for they loved the glory that comes from man more than the glory that comes from God*' (John 12:42-43, italics mine). This brings us back full circle. Idolatry robs God of His glory. When we fear others, we are seeking glory from others rather than the glory of God.

What our Children Think

'I hate you!' These are searing words for anyone to hear, but especially so for a parent. Perhaps your child has shouted these words to you in anger because you said no to something they wanted to do. Hearing such words from someone we have loved and cared for since before they were born is hurtful. More than hurtful. It cuts into the very heart of what it means to be a mother.

Motherhood is about sacrifice. It is the giving of life. For some moms, our child is created within our own bodies; we nurture them in our womb until they are ready

---

1. Welch, Edward, *What Do You Think of Me? Why Do I Care?* (Greensboro, NC: New Growth Press, 2011), Kindle edition: Location 16.

to be born. Other moms have gone to great lengths and labor to bring an orphan into their life and heart. We spend the next two decades of our life feeding, caring, teaching, training, and sacrificing for them. It's hard to hear ingratitude and hateful speech from someone to whom you've given so much of yourself.

For many, ingratitude or hateful words will sting and we will rightly be bothered by it. For others, it pierces at their very meaning and significance. We think we deserve more. Our children should be appreciative for all we've done for them. How dare they respond in that way? Paul Tripp cautions, 'Children should appreciate their parents. Yet, hear me now mothers and fathers—being appreciated cannot be our goal. When it becomes the thing we live for, we'll unwittingly look with hyper-vigilant eyes for appreciation in every situation.'[2]

The idol of approval is our 'god.' All gods are rulers and the god of approval is no different. Whoever we desire approval from the most is the one we will obey. This may look like people-pleasing—doing whatever it takes to get an approval response. In the case of our children, we want that 'I hate you!' to turn into 'You're the best Mommy ever!' and so we seek to please our child, giving them whatever they ask. Perhaps we discard the rules and limits. We may overlook things. We might even use money to buy their affection. Our children then become the kings and queens of our home; what they say goes. Our disordered desire for approval then creates a disordered home life.

---

2. Paul Tripp Ministries. https://www.paultripp.com/articles/posts/the-idol-of-appreciation (accessed June 10, 2017).

While we all swell with love and warmth when our children say 'Thank you, Mommy' or 'I love you, Mom' we can't live for those statements. Our children's thoughts, just like the thoughts of others, cannot be the factor that determines our value and worth. Like all idols, the idol of approval is a broken cistern.

Broken Cisterns

The prophet Jeremiah was called to warn God's people that judgment was coming. They had turned from God to worship false gods. Jeremiah was not a popular prophet. His call to repentance was met with opposition and persecution. The people were so angry with him; they even put him down into the bottom of a well to die (Jer. 38).

In Jeremiah 2, God tells Jeremiah to speak to the people. He begins by describing the past, 'I remember the devotion of your youth, your love as a bride, how you followed me in the wilderness, in a land not sown' (Jer. 2:2). Here again, we see God referring to His people in intimate terms, as a bride. He then asked, 'What wrong did your fathers find in me that they went far from me, and went after worthlessness, and became worthless? They did not say, "Where is the LORD who brought us up from the land of Egypt, who led us in the wilderness, in a land of desert and pits, in a land of drought and deep darkness, in a land that none passes through, where no man dwells?"' (Jer. 2:5-6). Israel forgot all that God had done for them in the wilderness and turned to worthless things, and by doing so, became worthless themselves. 'But my people have changed their glory for that which does not profit' (Jer. 2:11).

Their idolatry is serious; it is horrifying. 'Be appalled, O heavens, at this; be shocked, be utterly desolate, declares the LORD, for my people have committed two evils: they have forsaken me, the fountain of living waters, and hewed out cisterns for themselves, broken cisterns that can hold no water' (Jer. 2:12-13).

When we worship the idol of approval, we forsake God. We turn from our source of approval and acceptance and turn elsewhere to find approval. It is like seeking friendship in the voice of our computer's search engine rather than in a flesh and blood friend.

Everything else apart from God is a broken cistern. It cannot provide us what we really need. In the Bible, a cistern was a man-made well, shaped out of rock.[3] Some were rather large and used to hold water for an entire community. Empty and unused cisterns were often used to hold prisoners, such as the one Joseph was dropped into. Sometimes the cistern developed a crack, allowing water to leak. Like a cracked cistern that no longer holds water, seeking approval from others never fills us; it is always leaking out. It is a thirst that is never quenched.

Do you notice the stark contrast between what God provides in Jeremiah 2 and what we make for ourselves? What God offers us is a fountain, an endless supply of His love, acceptance, approval, and grace; what we create for ourselves is cracked and broken. Useless. Worthless.

Seeking approval from others or from our children will never satisfy. It is difficult to gain and impossible to keep.

---

3. Bible Hub. http://biblehub.com/topical/c/cistern.htm (accessed June 10, 2017).

We'll always live with the constant fear of what they think of us.

What matters most is what God thinks of us.

What God Thinks of Us

One of my favorite books is a little book. It's only four chapters but there is a lot packed into those four chapters. Tim Keller's book, *The Freedom of Self-Forgetfulness*, is important to our discussion about the idol of approval for it helps us learn to think rightly about ourselves. In thinking rightly about ourselves, we can then think rightly about what others think of us. The book is about humility and how the gospel shapes our self-worth and identity.

Society would tell us that we shouldn't care what others think of us; we should only care what we think of ourselves. This is pride. Our culture would say that we need to look at our accomplishments and see how great we are. We should decide who we want to be, what we want to do, and set off to achieve those things. When we've done so, we alone should be the ones who evaluate what we've done, not anyone else.

But the Bible looks at it differently. Instead of looking to others for approval or looking inward to ourselves for approval, Scripture points us upward, to Jesus. 'He took the condemnation we deserve; He faced the trial that should be ours so that we do not have to face any more trials. So I simply need to ask God to accept me because of what the Lord Jesus has done. Then, the only person whose opinion counts looks at me and He finds me more valuable than all the jewels in the earth.[4]

Tim Keller says that because our worth and identity is rooted in what Christ has done for us and in what God now thinks of us, we can have what he calls 'self-forgetfulness.' He wrote, 'the essence of gospel-humility is not thinking more of myself or thinking less of myself, it is thinking of myself less ... A truly gospel-humble person is not a self-hating person or a self-loving person, but a gospel-humble person. The truly gospel-humble person is a self-forgetful person whose ego is just like his or her toes. It just works. It does not draw attention to itself. The toes just work; the ego just works. Neither draws attention to itself.'[5]

When it comes to the idol of approval, we have to perform to get the approval, to get the good opinion and acceptance from those from whom we desire it. But with the gospel, we get the acceptance first. We hear God say that we are His beloved. We get Jesus' perfect performance. We are approved and accepted by God without any performance of our own. Now that we have the approval, we can perform based on what Christ has done. We can love others. We can serve. We can enjoy God's goodness. All because we are already approved and accepted in Christ.

Gospel Truth: God's Love for Us

While the approval and acceptance of others comes and goes, God's love for us is secure. There is nothing and no one who can separate us from Him. 'For I am sure that

---

4. Keller, Timothy, *The Freedom of Self-Forgetfulness* (Lancashire, England: 10ofThose, 2012), Kindle edition: Location 353.

5. Ibid, Location 277-87.

neither death nor life, nor angels nor rulers, nor things present nor things to come, nor powers, nor height nor depth, nor anything else in all creation, will be able to separate us from the love of God in Christ Jesus our Lord' (Rom. 8:38-39).

His love for us began in eternity past when He chose us in Christ. Through Christ, He adopted us as His own. We are beloved children of the Father and have all the benefits of a child of the King. As His children, we don't have to fear. 'For all who are led by the Spirit of God are sons of God. For you did not receive the spirit of slavery to fall back into fear, but you have received the Spirit of adoption as sons, by whom we cry, "Abba! Father!"' (Rom. 8:14-15).

As our Father, God knows what we need before we do. He hears all our cries and catches our tears. All the hairs of our head are numbered. 'Are not two sparrows sold for a penny? And not one of them will fall to the ground apart from your Father. But even the hairs of your head are all numbered. Fear not, therefore; you are of more value than many sparrows' (Matt. 10:29-31).

In fact, because we are united to Christ, God loves us as much as He loves His Son, 'I in them and you in me, that they may become perfectly one, so that the world may know that you sent me and loved them even as you loved me' (John 17:23). Stop for a moment and consider what this means. God loves us as much as He loves the Son. What wonder! Can you wrap your brain around that? It's too much! Infinite grace is what it is.

We are loved by the Maker of all things. He approves of us. The approval of others falls flat in comparison. What others think or say about us can never measure up to God's holy, perfect, and infinite love. The idol of approval never lasts; it is like chasing after the wind. God's love is forever. The idol of approval depends upon our performance. Our children's approval is dependent upon our actions. The approval of others changes depending on whether they like what we've done or not. But God's love and acceptance of us is based on Christ and His perfect performance on our behalf. His love will never wane or fluctuate; it is steady, constant, and sure.

When we worship the idol of approval, we are living like a fatherless orphan. It's like we've forgotten who we are. We've left the King's castle and are living on the street, content with the scraps others give us. All the while, the riches of the Kingdom are within reach. Love immeasurable is ours but we insist on digging in the trash pile. Friends, when the idol of approval tempts you, remember whose you are. Remember your standing in Christ and what God thinks of you. Remember your adoption. Remember you are loved.

Questions for a Mother's Heart:

1. Do you worship the idol of approval? In what ways does your sense of meaning and value come from what other people, including your children, think of you?

2. What relationship does the fear of man have with the idol of approval? What are some examples of ways you have feared what others think of you?

3. Read Jeremiah 2. How does God describe Israel's idolatry? What are the consequences?

4. Read Luke 15. What do these three parables tell you about God's love for you? What lengths does He go to in His love for you?

A Prayer for a Mother's Heart:

Father,

For so long I have desired and sought after approval from others. Now that I am a mother, I find myself doing it again. I care so much what others think of me. I fear they won't like me and will find me lacking.

But the truth is, you love me and accept me. I am your child whom you smile over. I am accepted in Christ. No matter what anyone else thinks of me, your thoughts about me will never waver or change.

Forgive me for finding my worth and meaning in what others think. Forgive me for the lengths I have gone to in gaining such approval. Forgive me for turning to others to receive what only you can give me.

Help me to dwell on who I am in Christ. Help me to remember your great love for me which is older than time itself. I thank you that though I wander, you always come after me and though I get lost, you always find me.

In Jesus' name,

Amen.

PART 3:

TURNING
FROM IDOLATRY

10

TURNING FROM OUR IDOLS

In the beginning of this book, I talked about how the unique challenges of motherhood give us an opportunity to see our sin in a new light. Motherhood can be hard. There's much that causes us to worry and fear. Motherhood is also challenging and stretching. It might even be different than we expected. In those difficulties, we often turn to idols for life and hope. In the preceding chapters, I touched on a few idols moms might worship, but there are certainly more than those few. Since anything can be an idol, there isn't a book which could describe them all.

I hope that as you've gone through this book, you've seen your heart and the idols you worship in a way you never have before. Perhaps you've felt the sting of the

Spirit's conviction. Maybe you've felt grief for the way you've turned from your first love—your Maker and Creator—to false loves. You may wonder—now what? Once we see and recognize the ways we look for life, hope, and meaning in created things rather than in God, what do we do? And most importantly, how do we defeat our idols?

This chapter and the next address just that.

Heart Awareness

In my family, heart disease is hereditary. I lost one relative to a heart attack and saw another go through quadruple bypass surgery. At a certain age, it seems like everyone in my family starts to show the signs. Annual blood work will reveal an increase in cholesterol. Blood pressure will start to rise. Plaque starts to build up in the arteries. At each stage, physicians advise and help us do what it takes to have a healthy heart.

For those who have heart disease, there are both preventative measures to keep the heart healthy as well as medical procedures to clean out clogged arteries and prevent heart attack. Exercise and diet are important. Adding healthy fats, like fish, is encouraged. A doctor might recommend supplements to increase good fats or medications to lower cholesterol. When necessary, doctors might recommend procedures (like inserting a stent to open an artery) or an invasive surgery (like a bypass surgery).

Heart disease is such an important medical issue that in America, there is an entire month dedicated to its awareness. Teaching and educating the public about the signs, symptoms, and treatment of heart disease goes a long way in promoting heart health and preventing heart attacks.

In a similar way, when it comes to our non-physical hearts, the core of who we are, we also need awareness. We need to understand the condition of our hearts. We need to know our tendency to erect and worship idols. We need to look deep into our hearts and see the idols we've established on the throne of our hearts. That's part of what this book has been about: to help us have a growing awareness of our idolatry.

Like our physical health, such awareness is not a one-time thing. We wouldn't go to the doctor for a check-up, learn we have a health problem that needs treatment, and then never return. We go to the doctor for regular check-ups, for maintenance and treatment of current conditions, and to test for new health problems. The same is true for our spiritual lives. We may realize that we worship the idol of control today but next year discover we have turned to worship the idol of success. As long as we live in this fallen world, as long as sin exists, we will battle against idolatry. Therefore we need to remain vigilant and watchful of our hearts.

The first step is heart awareness. We need an awareness of the contents of our own hearts. Take time to explore your thoughts, emotions, motivations, longings, and desires. Go through the list in chapter 4 and use it to evaluate your heart. If you remain uncertain about the idolatry of your heart, take the time now to pray and ask the Spirit to reveal it to you. Pray David's words, 'Search me, O God, and know my heart! Try me and know my thoughts!

And see if there be any grievous way in me, and lead me in the way everlasting!' (Ps. 139:23-24).

Remove Idols

Perhaps as you read this book, you realized right away the idols you worship. Whenever we identify sin in our lives, we need to confess our sin and receive God's forgiveness. 'If we confess our sins, he is faithful and just to forgive us our sins and to cleanse us from all unrighteousness' (1 John 1:9). David confirmed this promise is true, 'I acknowledged my sin to you, and I did not cover my iniquity; I said, "I will confess my transgressions to the LORD," and you forgave the iniquity of my sin' (Ps. 32:5). All our sins are washed clean by the blood of our Savior.

Confession involves honesty. We are honest with ourselves and with God. We freely admit what we've done. We don't excuse it or blame others for it. We don't call it less than it is. We describe it and name it for the true evil that it is. Such confession also involves humility. We have to humble ourselves before the Lord. We have to recognize that God is God and we are not. Our sin is against a holy and righteous God and is deserving of death. And then we relish the grace that is lavished upon us in Christ.

When it comes to the sin of idolatry, we don't just confess to being an idolater; we confess the specific idols we've bowed down to. We confess the sacrifices we've made to our idols, the sins we've committed to keep and maintain those idols, and the way we've prostrated our hearts to something created rather than to our Creator. We confess the sinful longings and desires of our heart, our emotional responses when our idols have been threatened, and the ways we've sought hope and joy apart from God.

Confession is always accompanied by repentance, the turning away from sin. We don't just say we are sorry and then continue to walk the same path. We have to turn away from our idols. We have to remove them from our hearts. Elise Fitzpatrick wrote, 'True repentance involves a hatred for sin and a turning from it and from all self-salvation projects ... It's only as I hate my sin that I'll have the desire to fight it.'[1]

Turning away from sin often involves a serious and dramatic response. Jesus said in the book of Matthew: 'If your right eye causes you to sin, tear it out and throw it away. For it is better that you lose one of your members than that your whole body be thrown into hell. And if your right hand causes you to sin, cut it off and throw it away. For it is better that you lose one of your members than that your whole body go into hell' (Matt. 5:29-30). Jesus is using hyperbole here for effect. And it does have an effect, doesn't it? What this passage means is that sin is serious and we should treat it seriously. Sometimes it means taking some drastic measures with our sin. For example, it may mean staying away from specific stores, turning off the television, getting rid of certain books, and closing down social media accounts. It may mean seeking accountability from others. It should mean sharing and confessing those sins with a trusted gospel friend, for only when we bring sin out into the light do we see it for what

---

1. Fitzpatrick, Elise M., *Idols of the Heart: Learning to Long for God Alone*, Revised Edition (Phillipsburg, NJ: P&R Publishing, 2016), p. 201.

it truly is. It will definitely mean capturing sinful thoughts and making them obedient to Christ. It will also mean digging our idols up by their roots and getting rid of them. 'Therefore, my beloved, flee from idolatry' (1 Cor. 10:14).

Paul compares this to how an athlete trains his body to run a race. 'Do you not know that in a race all the runners run, but only one receives the prize? So run that you may obtain it. Every athlete exercises self-control in all things. They do it to receive a perishable wreath, but we an imperishable. So I do not run aimlessly; I do not box as one beating the air. But I discipline my body and keep it under control, lest after preaching to others I myself should be disqualified' (1 Cor. 9:24-27). Anyone who has trained for a marathon understands this analogy. But if you are not a runner (I'm not), consider the work and discipline you have put into another area of your life, whether it is a career goal, a financial goal, an educational goal, or some other pursuit for which you worked hard. We are to train and work just as hard in putting our sin to death.

This self-control is not like the self-control of the world. It is not produced by trying harder and believing in the self; rather, it is a fruit of the Spirit (Gal. 5:23). It is a God-given, grace-driven self-control. Such control is powered by Christ. Paul wrote in Colossians that he toils, but through the energy of Christ, 'For this I toil, struggling with all his energy that he powerfully works within me' (Col. 1:29). We fight sin and idolatry with all that we have, but not in our own strength; we fight it through the power of God at work in us. 'But if Christ is in you, although the body is dead because of sin, the Spirit is life because of righteousness ... For if you live according to the flesh you will die, but if by the Spirit you put to death the deeds of the body, you will live. For all who are led by the Spirit of God are sons of God' (Rom. 8:10, 13-14). And the goal of this self-control is not an earthly prize or honor but God's glory, honor, and fame.

Guard the Heart

Like our physical hearts, we need to guard our spiritual hearts. We need to keep watch over them. We need to do regular heart checks. We need to be aware of our tendencies to worship false gods, and watch out for them. 'Keep your heart with all vigilance, for from it flow the springs of life' (Prov. 4:23).

Sinclair Ferguson once created a catechism on the heart in an article he wrote for *Tabletalk Magazine*. Using a catechism format, he created questions and answers about the heart. One such question and answer was:

Q: What four things does God counsel me to do so that my heart may be kept for Him?

A: First, I must guard my heart as if everything depended on it. This means that I should keep my heart like a sanctuary for the presence of the Lord Jesus and allow nothing and no one else to enter.

Second, I must keep my heart healthy by proper diet, growing strong on a regular diet of God's Word— reading it for myself, meditating on its truth, but especially being fed on it in the preaching of the Word. I also will remember that my heart has eyes as well as ears. The Spirit shows me baptism as a sign that I bear God's triune name, while the Lord's Supper stimulates heart love for the Lord Jesus.

Third, I must take regular spiritual exercise, since my heart will be strengthened by worship when my whole being is given over to God in expressions of love for and trust in Him.

Fourth, I must give myself to prayer in which my heart holds on to the promises of God, rests in His will, and asks for His sustaining grace—and do this not only on my own but with others so that we may encourage one another to maintain a heart for God.[2]

We guard our hearts from worshipping idols by learning, knowing, memorizing, and meditating on God's Word. The Word is powerful. It is truth which sanctifies (John 17:17). When we read and study Scripture, it will get down deep into our heart. It will discern our longings and desires, our idols and false loves. The more we read, the more the Spirit will use it to convict us of sin and change and transform us into the image of Christ. 'For the word of God is living and active, sharper than any two-edged sword, piercing to the division of soul and of spirit, of joints and of marrow, and discerning the thoughts and intentions of the heart' (Heb. 4:12).

God's Word is also our life. Moses told the people before they entered the promised land, 'Take to heart all the words by which I am warning you today, that you may command them to your children, that they may be careful to do all the words of this law. For it is no empty word for you, *but your very life*, and by this word you shall live long in the land that you are going over the Jordan to possess'

---

2. Ferguson, Sinclair, 'A Catechism on the Heart' *Tabletalk Magazine,* (January 2012), p. 65.

(Deut. 32:46-47, emphasis mine). It is like bread which feeds, nourishes, and sustains our soul.

We also guard our hearts when we worship the Lord, both privately and corporately. When we spend time dwelling on the goodness of God and responding to Him in praise and adoration, our hearts are focused on the true and living God, not false gods. We do this by taking time to respond in thanksgiving for the good gifts God has given us. Being intentional to turn to the Giver of all good things in gratitude helps keep our hearts focused on Him. Reading through the Psalms of praise and thanksgiving and making them our own is one way to do this.

In public worship, being faithful to join our church community each week and participating in the means of grace God has provided for us reminds us that worship is a holy and sacred event, reserved for the one true God. Hearing the Word preached, receiving communion, singing praise with our brothers and sisters, praying for the needs of others, and participating in corporate confession on the Lord's Day strengthens us to fight sin and live out the gospel.

As Ferguson noted, we also need to devote ourselves to prayer. We can't fight the sin of idolatry on our own; we need His grace. We need to be in constant prayer, asking God to help us in this fight. We need to pray for wisdom and discernment to recognize our idols and know how to root them out. In our prayers, we need to focus our hearts on who God is and what He has done for us in Christ. We need to confess our idolatry in prayer and apply the gospel to our sin. Because we are part of the Body of Christ, we need to ask others to pray for us as well. We need to participate in community prayer and join our hearts together in unity, seeking God's will and mercy in our lives.

An Ongoing Battle

As I pointed out earlier, though Christ has conquered the power of sin in our lives, the presence of sin still wages war in our hearts. Though we may do the things listed above (read the Bible, pray, worship), we will still find ourselves turning to idols to fill emptiness, to meet the longings of our hearts. Indeed, this fight against idolatry will be a lifetime battle. As Elise Fitzpatrick wrote, 'Even as believers, with new hearts and renewed desires, it is impossible that any of us will perfectly love God with our whole heart, soul, mind, and strength because of remaining sin and our unbelief. Our hearts will always be drawn away to things we can see, taste, and touch, drawn away to something more than faith in the unseen. We will always be tempted to choose to worship something other than God, to love something more than we love Him, to swear our allegiance to other deities—whether to ourselves as our own savior or to someone or something else we think has the power to make us truly happy.'[3] This is the reality of Christian life in a fallen world. Paul expressed this vividly in Romans 7: 'For I do not understand my own actions. For I do not do what I want, but I do the very thing I hate' (v. 15).

It can be discouraging. Some days, it seems like we are fighting a losing battle. Just when we think we've turned from an idol, we find ourselves worshipping another. It can be tempting to give up or to think God has given up

---

3. Fitzpatrick, Elise, p. 167.

on us. But Paul gives us hope, 'Wretched man that I am! Who will deliver me from this body of death? Thanks be to God through Jesus Christ our Lord!' (Rom. 7:24-25). Christ defeated sin for us. He is our deliverer. In our fight against idolatry, Christ is the victor. We have to look to Him each and every day for grace and be washed anew in the gospel. We have to remember that we are not alone, the Lord is with us even in our hardest days, and He never lets go of us.

There is joy even in the midst of the battle. 'You can rejoice because the Lord Jesus has already triumphed over your sin on the cross, and one day you will be completely free. But at the same time, you can seek to guard against the deceptive thoughts, desires, or inclinations of your heart. You can fight against unbelief and continually throw yourself on the mercy of God.[4] God is rich in mercy and His mercy and grace towards us keeps us and sustains us in the fight.

In fact, God doesn't call us to fight against sin and then not provide us the resources to fight against it. He doesn't leave us on our own in this battle. 2 Peter tells us God has given us everything we need to live for Him, 'His divine power has granted to us all things that pertain to life and godliness, through the knowledge of him who called us to his own glory and excellence' (2 Pet. 1:3). He doesn't leave us empty-handed; He supplies us with everything we need. He gives us His Spirit who works in us to will and to act according to His purposes for us (Phil. 2:13).

---

4. Ibid.

Even at our weakest moments when it doesn't seem possible that we will ever win the battle against idolatry, the Spirit is at work in us, remaking us, molding and shaping us. Nothing will keep Him from fulfilling His will for us: 'For we are his workmanship, created in Christ Jesus for good works, which God prepared beforehand, that we should walk in them' (Eph. 2:10). Not only that, but God *will* finish the work He began in us (Phil. 1:6). He will sustain us to the end (1 Cor. 1:8). That gives us hope in this fight. One day we will cross the finish line and receive the crown of life. We'll be holy, perfect, and complete, a beautiful reflection of our Savior. I certainly long for that day, don't you?

Questions for a Mother's Heart:

1. Read Ephesians 4:17-32. According to Paul, what does our old life look like before Christ? What does it look like now?

2. Read Colossians 3:1-17. What does Paul say to put off? What does he say to put on? And why can we do that? (hint: reread verses 1 and 3).

3. Read David's confession in Psalm 51 and make it your own.

4. Make a list of things you can thank God for today. Then pray through that list, worshipping God for His goodness and faithfulness to you in Christ.

A Prayer for a Mother's Heart:

Father in heaven,

I see more and more of my true heart condition. Holy Spirit, thank you for helping me to see the idols in my heart. Help me to grow more and more aware of what's in my heart. I pray that you would help me to put off my old self and put on new life in Christ.

Forgive me for not feasting on the Word. Forgive me for not praying. Forgive me for not guarding my heart. I pray that I would stay in this battle and fight the sin of idolatry. May I use the means you've provided to feed and nourish my heart with truth and grace.

I rejoice that because of Jesus, you will finish what you started in me. You will make me like Christ. You will remove all my sin. I thank you that one day this battle will be over. Come quickly, Lord Jesus!

In Jesus' sweet name I pray,

Amen.

11

TURNING TO CHRIST

When my kids were young, I taught them the concept of repentance by having them jump up and turn away from facing one wall to face the opposite wall instead. To repent of sin, not only do we turn away from wrongdoing, we turn instead to something else—someone else: God.

In the last chapter, we talked about turning from our idols and uprooting them from our hearts. We also looked at heart health and specific steps we can take to guard our hearts from idolatry. All of those things are good and important things to do. But they can't be done apart from what we are going to talk about in this chapter: turning *to* Christ.

Tim Keller says that the only way to remove an idol is to replace it with greater love for Christ. He wrote, 'Jesus must become more beautiful to your imagination, more attractive to your heart, than your idol. That is what will replace your counterfeit gods. If you uproot the idol and fail to "plant" the love of Christ in its place, the idol will grow back.'[1] Christ must become our treasure, what we love and value more than anything else. Otherwise, if we remove an idol and fail to turn to Christ, we'll just replace the idol we removed with another idol.

We've all probably had that experience in our faith at some point. For example, perhaps we realized we had grown materialistic and spent too much time focusing on accumulating things. We were consumed with having the latest gadgets and fashions. Over time, we discovered we were going into debt to feed our materialism. We were convicted and repented. But rather than replace the love of things with the love of Christ, we turned to something else. Perhaps we went the opposite direction and purged our possessions and chose to live simply. But then we found ourselves looking down on others who have material possessions. It's easy to swing from one idol to another—in this case going from the idol of materialism to that of simplicity.

Sometimes we don't vacillate at all and instead replace our idol with something else entirely. Perhaps we uprooted the idol of comfort and stopped bingeing on television. But before long, we found another and different love. Perhaps it was health and we became consumed with working

1. Keller, Timothy, *Counterfeit Gods: The Empty Promises of Money, Sex, and Power, and the Only Hope that Matters* (New York, NY: Dutton, 2009), p. 172.

out and eating certain foods. Or maybe it was our work we turned to instead, where we focused on being successful in our field. Everyone's idol is different but we all respond the same way—if we are not worshipping Christ, we will worship something.

So how does Christ become our treasure? How do we love and worship Him rather than turning to another idol?

To Know Him is to Love Him

When you first meet a new friend or begin a dating rela tionship, if you enjoy the person's company, you look for more opportunities to be with that person. Perhaps you talk about shared likes and common interests. You might talk about childhood experiences and what you do with your time. As time moves on and the longer you know the other person, you might begin talking about your hopes and dreams, past heartaches and sorrows, and what kind of person you long to be. The more you know the other person, the more you care about them.

In a similar way, the more we know Christ, the more we grow in our love for Him. This happens as we learn about His character and who He is. It happens as we learn more about what He has done in our lives and in the lives of others. It happens as we listen to what He has to say and learn about what is important to Him. It happens as we stand in His presence and experience His grace rain down upon us.

Like any other relationship, we have to spend time with Christ in order to know Him. The best way to do that is by reading and studying His Word. The Bible tells us all we need to know about Him. We can read His spoken words in the gospels. We can read the testimony of those who spent time with Him in the epistles and pastoral letters. We can read the promises and prophecies of what He would do and who He would be in the Old Testament. If you want to know Christ, read the Bible. And in knowing Christ, you will know God.

Jesus made many statements telling us who He is, including many 'I am' statements in the book of John. It's worth reading what He has to say about Himself.

He is the light of the world: 'I am the light of the world. Whoever follows me will not walk in darkness, but will have the light of life' (John 8:12).

He is the bread of life: 'I am the bread of life; whoever comes to me shall not hunger, and whoever who believes in me shall never thirst' (John 6:35).

He is the way, the truth, the life: 'I am the way, and the truth, and the life. No one comes to the Father except through me' (John 14:6).

He is the good shepherd: 'I am the good shepherd. The good shepherd lays down his life for the sheep' (John 10:11).

He is the resurrection: 'I am the resurrection and the life. Whoever believes in me, though he die, yet shall he live, and everyone who lives and believes in me shall never die' (John 11:25-26).

He is the vine: 'I am the vine; you are the branches. Whoever abides in me and I in him, he it is that bears much fruit, for apart from me you can do nothing' (John 15:5).

He is God: 'Truly, truly, I say to you, before Abraham was, I am' (John 8:58).

The Bible also teaches us about what Christ has done. All of these truths make up the good news of the gospel, the foundation of our faith.

He lived a perfect life: 'For we do not have a high priest who is unable to sympathize with our weaknesses, but one who in every respect has been tempted as we are, yet without sin' (Heb. 4:15).

He became sin for us: 'For our sake he made him to be sin who knew no sin, so that in him we might become the righteousness of God' (2 Cor. 5:21).

He died for us: 'But he was pierced for our transgressions; he was crushed for our iniquities; upon him was the chastisement that brought us peace, and with his wounds we are healed (Isa. 53:5).

He was raised for us: '…who was delivered up for our trespasses and raised for our justification' (Rom. 4:25).

He gave us His Spirit: 'And I will ask the Father, and he will give you another Helper, to be with you forever, even the Spirit of truth, whom the world cannot receive, because it neither sees him nor knows him. You know him, for he dwells with you and will be in you' (John 14: 16-17).

He intercedes for us: 'Christ Jesus is the one who died— more than that, who was raised—who is at the right hand of God, who indeed is interceding for us' (Rom. 8:34).

He is preparing for us a place in eternity: 'And if I go and prepare a place for you, I will come again and will take you to myself, that where I am you may be also' (John 14:3).

These truths about Christ and who He is are truths into which we need to steep our hearts. We need to dwell and meditate on them. We need to rehearse them in our minds every moment. Some call it 'preaching the gospel' to ourselves. The more we dwell on these truths, the more we realize God's love for us in Christ, the more our idols will shrink in comparison. 'Our hearts are only weaned from our idols by the power of a stronger love, the power of the Father's love for us in the gospel.'[2]

The marvelous wonder and grace of the gospel is not that we keep a tight grip onto God but that He holds onto us. Because we are sinful and fallen, there will be times when we forget these truths. We will forget who He is and what He has done. We will fail to love Him with all our hearts and will instead erect counterfeit gods to love and serve. But God never lets go of us. Our security is not based on how strong our faith is or how often we read the Bible or how much we love God; rather, it rests in Christ's work for us. It is His grip which holds us secure, not our grip on Him. 'For I am sure that neither death nor life, nor angels nor rulers, nor things present nor things to come, nor powers, nor height nor depth, nor anything else in all creation, will be able to separate us from the love of God in Christ Jesus our Lord' (Rom. 8:38-39). Nothing can stop God's love for us, not even our weak and fickle faith, nor our idolatrous hearts.

Rejoice in this truth, dear friends. God's mercy is new and fresh each day. When you stand firm against idolatry, give thanks to God for His grace which enables you to stand. When you stumble and turn to an idol, repent and rest in the gospel of grace which rescues you. And every day, turn to Christ in love and thanksgiving for who He is and what He has done for you.

---

2. Fitzpatrick, Elise M., *Idols of the Heart: Learning to Long for God Alone*, Revised Edition (Phillipsburg, NJ: P&R Publishing, 2016), p. 217.

Responding in Worship

Whatever we desire and long for is what we will worship. We've learned that in our study of idolatry. That's why understanding God's great love for us in Christ is so important. The more we know of God's love, the more we can't help but respond in love, praise, and thanksgiving. As we turn to God in awe and wonder for what He has done, we will worship Him instead of false idols.

Elise Fitzpatrick notes, 'A heart that is crammed with thoughts of God's beauty, kindness, holiness, majesty, glory, and grace has no room for counterfeits and will inevitably burst forth with fervent praises.'[3] As the psalmist wrote, 'I have stored up your word in my heart, that I might not sin against you' (Ps. 119:11). What we fill our hearts with will overflow into our actions and into our worship.

The book of Psalms is the worship book of the Bible. It's the hymnal the Israelites used in their worship, just as we sing our hymns and spiritual songs in church today. The Psalms were used in all seasons of life, from the good times to the bad, from the fearful and tumultuous times to the joy-filled and peaceful times. No matter what was going on in the life of God's people, there was a song to sing to God.

The Psalms teach us a lot about our own worship and I don't just mean formal worship on Sunday mornings. I mean the leanings, longings, and desires of our heart. The Psalms show us how to train our hearts to turn to God in thanksgiving and praise. They give us words to

---

3. Ibid., p. 226.

sing in our hearts to God. They remind us of what is true. They glorify and exalt God and help us see more of His wonder and majesty. The Psalms help us treasure God.

Theologians often group the individual psalms into genres or types of psalms. That's because the individual psalms often have different tones and purposes. But there is something we can learn from all the psalms about worshipping and praising God. Though there are a few different genres, I'm going to focus on three.

When life was going well, the Israelites sang songs of praise.[4] These songs focused on what God had done in the past, most notably their rescue from slavery in Egypt. They also speak about God as Creator, sustainer, and provider of all things. In Psalm 68:7-8 the psalmist wrote, 'O God, when you went out before your people, when you marched through the wilderness, the earth quaked, the heavens poured down rain, before God, the One of Sinai, before God, the God of Israel.' We too can praise God for our own deliverance as we dwell on what Christ did for us at the cross and how He rescued us from our sin. In Psalm 33, the psalmist praised God for the works and wonders He has made, 'By the word of the LORD the heavens were made, and by the breath of his mouth all their host. He gathers the waters of the sea as a heap; he puts the deeps in storehouses. Let all the earth fear the LORD; let all the inhabitants of the world stand in awe of him! For he spoke, and it came to be; he commanded, and it stood firm' (vv. 6-9). Consider

---

4. For more about the Psalms, I recommend *Joy Comes in the Morning: Psalms for All Seasons* by Mark Futato (Phillipsburg, NJ: P&R Publishing, 2004).

God's creation and the works of His hands. Praise Him and adore Him as Creator.

The Israelites sang songs of thanksgiving when God had rescued and delivered them from an immediate trouble or trial. In Psalm 18, David wrote about God delivering him from the hands of Saul. He praised and thanked God for being his refuge. 'He rescued me from my strong enemy and from those who hated me, for they were too mighty for me. They confronted me in the day of my calamity, but the LORD was my support. He brought me out into a broad place; he rescued me, because he delighted in me' (vv. 17-19).

The psalms of thanksgiving often invite and tell others of the good news of what God has done. 'I have told the glad news of deliverance in the great congregation; behold, I have not restrained my lips, as you know, O LORD. I have not hidden your deliverance within my heart; I have spoken of your faithfulness and your salvation; I have not concealed your steadfast love and your faithfulness from the great congregation' (Ps. 40:9-10). We have much to thank God for in our lives, and all too often fail to do so. Take time to consider and dwell on God's goodness to you each day and thank Him for it. Tell others of God's goodness and invite them to rejoice with you.

Even the darkest psalms, the laments, turn to God in thanksgiving, praise, and worship. These are the psalms written by those who were filled with fear, sorrow, or despair. The writers often felt forgotten by God, but still they cried out to God and asked for help and deliverance. In the laments, the writers often referred to God as their refuge, rock, and deliverer. In doing so, they reminded themselves of who God is and His faithfulness towards them. 'The LORD is my light and my salvation; whom shall I fear? The LORD is the stronghold of my life; of whom shall I be afraid?' (Ps. 27:1). Nearly all the laments end with a response of trust and worship. The psalmists might not have yet received an answer to their prayers but as they turned to God, crying out to Him for rescue and help, they knew He heard them and would respond. 'But I have trusted in your steadfast love; my heart shall rejoice in your salvation. I will sing to the LORD, because he has dealt bountifully with me' (Ps. 13:5-6).[5]

Consider reading and studying the Psalms for yourself and use them to praise and worship God. Memorize and hide them in your heart. Use them to remind yourself of God's goodness and love for you.

Enjoying God

When we started this book, we began by looking at our purpose and why God made us. If you remember, I referred to the Westminster Confession and its definition of our purpose in life: to glorify God and enjoy Him forever.

Now that we have explored idolatry and specific idols of a mother's heart and looked at ways to root out such idols, we should end by returning to our chief end in life. When we fill our minds and hearts with thoughts of God's goodness, holiness, truth, wonder, and majesty we find ourselves turning away from our idols and back to the One who made

---

5. To read more about the laments, my book *A Heart Set Free: A Journey to Hope Through the Psalms of Lament* (Ross-Shire, Scotland: Christian Focus, 2016) is about applying the structure of the laments to your own prayer life.

us. Our restless hearts are finally stilled in the presence of Him who fills the chasm of our heart. As we enjoy God, who He is and what He has done, we then glorify Him. And we will live as the worshippers we were created to be.

Let me end with this Psalm from David. It is a good summary and reminder of the emptiness of idolatry and the source of true joy.

Psalm 16

Preserve me, O God, for in you I take refuge.
I say to the Lord, 'You are my Lord;
I have no good apart from you.'

As for the saints in the land, they are the excellent ones,
in whom is all my delight.

The sorrows of those who run after another god shall
multiply;
their drink offerings of blood I will not pour out
or take their names on my lips.

The Lord is my chosen portion and my cup;
you hold my lot.
The lines have fallen for me in pleasant places;
indeed, I have a beautiful inheritance.

I bless the Lord who gives me counsel;
in the night also my heart instructs me.
I have set the Lord always before me;
because he is at my right hand, I shall not be shaken.

Therefore my heart is glad, and my whole being
rejoices;

my flesh also dwells secure.
For you will not abandon my soul to Sheol,
or let your holy one see corruption.

You make known to me the path of life;
in your presence there is fullness of joy;
at your right hand are pleasures forevermore.

Questions for a Mother's Heart:

1. Why isn't confession and repentance enough to root out the idols in our hearts? What do we need to plant in our hearts instead?

2. Select two truths about Christ to meditate on today.

3. Read Psalm 33. What does the psalmist say about who God is and what He has done?

4. Read Psalm 119. How does the psalmist describe God's Word? Why does meditating on God's Word keep us from sin?

A Prayer for a Mother's Heart:

Father in heaven,

As I consider all these gospel truths of who Christ is and what He has done for me, I am blown over. Knocked to my knees. I am in silent awe and wonder-struck by your love and grace. I thank you and praise you for your great love. I thank you that it is not conditional upon my own love or actions but on your perfect love. Forgive me for not resting in the gospel. Forgive me for turning my eyes away from you. Hold me, sustain me, and keep me until that day when you return to take me home.

In Jesus' name,

Amen.

Christian Focus Publications

Our mission statement –

STAYING FAITHFUL

In dependence upon God we seek to impact the world through literature faithful to His infallible Word, the Bible. Our aim is to ensure that the Lord Jesus Christ is presented as the only hope to obtain forgiveness of sin, live a useful life and look forward to heaven with Him.

Our books are published in four imprints:

CHRISTIAN FOCUS

Popular works including biographies, commentaries, basic doctrine and Christian living.

CHRISTIAN HERITAGE

Books representing some of the best material from the rich heritage of the church.

MENTOR

Books written at a level suitable for Bible College and seminary students, pastors, and other serious readers. The imprint includes commentaries, doctrinal studies, examination of current issues and church history.

CF4•K

Children's books for quality Bible teaching and for all age groups: Sunday school curriculum, puzzle and activity books; personal and family devotional titles, biographies and inspirational stories – because you are never too young to know Jesus!

Christian Focus Publications Ltd,
Geanies House, Fearn, Ross-shire,
IV20 1TW, Scotland, United Kingdom.
www.christianfocus.com
blog.christianfocus.com